FARMSTAND FAVORITES

Tomatoes

Over 75 Farm Fresh Recipes

Farmstand Favorites: Tomatoes

Hatherleigh Press is committed to preserving and protecting the natural resources of the Earth. Environmentally responsible and sustainable practices are embraced within the company's mission statement.

Hatherleigh Press is a member of the Publishers Earth Alliance, committed to preserving and protecting the natural resources of the planet while developing a sustainable business model for the book publishing industry.

This book was edited and designed in the village of Hobart, New York. Hobart is a community that has embraced books and publishing as a component of its livelihood. There are several unique bookstores in the village. For more information, please visit www.hobartbookvillage.com.

DISCLAIMER
This book offers general cooking and eating suggestions for educational purposes only. In no case should it be a substitute nor replace a healthcare professional. Consult your healthcare professional to determine which foods are safe for you and to establish the right diet for your personal nutritional needs.

Library of Congress Cataloging-in-Publication Data is available upon request.
978-1-57826-411-7

All Hatherleigh Press titles are available for bulk purchase, special promotions, and premiums. For information about reselling and special purchase opportunities, please call 1-800-528-2550 and ask for the Special Sales Manager.

Cover and Interior Design by Nick Macagnone

10 9 8 7 6 5 4 3 2 1

Printed in the United States

Improve your life. Change your world.

Acknowledgments

Hatherleigh Press would like to extend a special thank you to Meghan Price and Christine Schultz—without your hard work and creativity this book would not have been possible.

Table of Contents

All About Tomatoes

The tomato is the fruit of the *Lycopersicon esculentum* plant. Due to its lack of sweetness, the tomato is considered a vegetable for culinary purposes. The tomato is native to Mexico and gets its name from the Aztecan word *tomatl* meaning "the swelling fruit." Despite its popularity in European cuisine, the tomato did not arrive in Europe until the 1500s, and for a long time, it was stigmatized as a member of the nightshade family. This family includes eggplant, bell peppers, potatoes, paprika, and other common edible plant products. Nightshade produce contain traces of alkaloids, which may adversely affect some individuals. However, most people can consume nightshade produce without any side effects. Italy was the first European country to embrace the tomato. In Italian, tomatoes are called *pomi d'oro,* meaning "golden apples." The French believed that the tomato had aphrodisiac powers and named it *pommes d'amour,* which translates as "love apples." Thanks to its versatility, the tomato is now popular in a variety of cuisines. Today, approximately 130 million tons of tomatoes are produced each year, with the United States as one of the top three producers.

For optimum taste, be sure to get tomatoes from your local farmstand in the summer and early fall. For maximum nutrients, choose richly colored tomatoes. Ripe tomatoes should exude a sweet aroma and be firm, yet yield slightly to pressure. Avoid buying tomatoes that are wrinkled, cracked, bruised, or puffy in appearance.

Health Benefits of Tomatoes

Tomatoes are rich in *antioxidants,* especially vitamin C, beta-carotene, manganese, and vitamin E. Antioxidants tame cancer-causing free radicals, and some studies suggest that tomatoes help fight cancer. The tomato's concentration of alpha-tomatine is especially effective in fighting prostate cancer. Research also suggests that carotenoid lycopene found in tomatoes may reduce the risk for breast cancer.

Because lycopene promotes bone health, studies have shown that lycopene reduces the risk of osteoporosis. Studies show that the antioxidant content of tomatoes also supports bone, liver, kidney, cardiovascular, and bloodstream health.

Tomatoes are especially great for your heart! The intake of fresh tomatoes and tomato extracts has been shown to lower total cholesterol, LDL (bad) cholesterol, and triglyceride levels. *Phytonutrients* in tomatoes (including carotenoids, flavinoids, hydroxycinnamic acids, glycosides, and fatty acid derivatives) prevent the aggregation, or clumping, of blood platelets. This is especially helpful in preventing atherosclerosis, which is the thickening of artery walls from a buildup of fats.

Other research suggests that those who have diets rich in tomatoes are less likely to develop Alzheimer's disease and other neurological diseases. Due to their low calorie content, tomatoes are also linked with a lowered risk of obesity.

Tomatoes contain many key nutrients including (in descending order):

- vitamin C
- vitamin A
- vitamin K
- potassium
- molybdenum
- manganese
- dietary fiber
- vitamin B6 (pyridoxine)
- folate
- copper
- vitamin B3 (niacin)
- magnesium
- vitamin E
- vitamin B1 (thiamin)
- phosphorus
- protein

- tryptophan
- choline
- iron

Varieties of Tomatoes

Although many think of the tomato as a plump red fruit, there are over a thousand varieties of tomatoes which come in different shapes, colors, and sizes! Some colors include yellow, orange, pink, green, purple, and even white. A few popular types of tomatoes include:

- **Cherry Tomatoes:** Bite-sized variety with a circular shape and sweet taste. Most commonly enjoyed in salads.
- **Plum Tomatoes:** An oblong variety with a higher ratio of solids, making them ideal for sauces.
- **Grape Tomatoes:** A smaller version of the plum tomato. Most commonly used in salads.
- **Heirloom Tomatoes:** A larger variety with higher resistance to disease. They are also self-pollinating and especially flavorful.
- **Beefsteak Tomatoes:** A kidney-shaped tomato, most commonly used in sandwiches. However, they have a shorter shelf life than other varieties.

Recent studies have shown that conventional and organic growing methods have little to no effect on a tomato's antioxidant content. Instead, tomato variety is the major determinant of antioxidant richness.

Ripening and Storing Tomatoes

For the best results, store your tomatoes at room temperature and out of direct sunlight. Depending on how ripe the tomatoes are when you purchase them, they can last about a week in this state.

Your tomatoes will not ripen properly in the refrigerator, but if you don't want them to get overripe, you may store them in the refrigerator. They will last about two days in this state, but they will lose their flavor and firmness. Remove from the refrigerator 30 minutes before use to get the maximum flavor and texture.

Tomato sauce, and even whole or chopped tomatoes, can be stored in the freezer if you plan to cook them later. Freeze tomatoes in plastic containers or plastic bags (never use aluminum foil since the acidity of the tomatoes will chemically react with the aluminum. See preparation tips for further information.). When freezing tomato sauce or paste, leave some empty space in the container to compensate for expansion. Store sun-dried tomatoes in an airtight container and keep them in a cool, dry place.

To hasten the ripening process, you can place tomatoes in a paper bag with an apple or a banana. These fruits emit ethylene gas, which aids in the maturation of tomatoes. However, tomatoes which ripen on the plant tend to be more flavorful and juicy.

Some Preparation Tips

Be sure to wash tomatoes in cool water and dry before incorporating them into any dish. To maximize nutritional value, use the entire tomato and do not dispose of the seeds or skin.

Because of the tomato's acidity, avoid cooking tomatoes with aluminum cookware. Not only will the tomatoes absorb the aluminum taste, but the aluminum may inversely affect your health.

Breakfast

Garden Vegetable Omelet with Cheese

Courtesy of Monica Musetti-Carlin, as seen in
Country Comfort: Summer Favorites
Serves 2–4

Ingredients:

1 cup yellow onion, diced fine
2 small zucchini, sliced thin
½ cup mushrooms, sliced thin
1 clove garlic, diced very fine
2 tablespoons butter
6 eggs, beaten with 1 tablespoon water
1 medium tomato, chopped
1 sprig parsley, chopped very fine
1 cup cheddar cheese, shredded
Sea salt and freshly cracked black pepper, to taste

Directions:

Sauté onion, zucchini, mushrooms, and garlic in 1 tablespoon of butter for 3–4 minutes and set aside. Melt remaining butter in large frying pan, and pour in beaten eggs, constantly pushing the egg mixture toward the center of the pan so the uncooked egg continues to fill the pan and cook. Once mostly cooked, shake the pan to loosen and carefully turn over. Immediately place onion, zucchini, mushrooms, garlic, tomato, half of the parsley, and cheese in the center of the egg. Turn half of the egg over the other, covering the vegetables, and then press gently with a spatula. Once the cheese begins to melt, turn the egg once, turn again if needed, and serve once all the cheese is melted. Sprinkle while hot off the stove with the remaining parsley and cheese. Salt and pepper to taste. (As an alternative to sautéing, you can also put the zucchini, onion, mushrooms, and butter in a microwave-safe bowl, cover with plastic wrap, and cook on high for 3 minutes before adding to the omelet.)

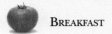

Tomato, Garlic, Crouton, and Pesto Omelet

Courtesy of the Florida Tomato Committee
(www.floridatomatoes.org)

Serves 1

Ingredients:

4 slices sturdy, white or whole-wheat bread

1 tablespoon olive oil

1 clove garlic, minced

2 large or extra-large eggs

1 teaspoon water

1 tablespoon unsalted butter

¼–⅓ cup grated mozzarella cheese

2 tablespoons homemade or store-bought pesto

1 large tomato, cut into bite-size chunks

Salt, to taste

Directions:

Preheat the oven to 300°F. Cut the bread into cubes and toss in a bowl with the oil and garlic. Spread the cubes on a baking sheet and toast them for 15 to 25 minutes, until golden brown. Transfer to a plate to cool.

When you are ready to make the omelet, have all the ingredients nearby. Crack the eggs into a small bowl, add the water and salt, and beat lightly.

Place a nonstick omelet pan over medium-high heat and add the butter. When it starts to sizzle, add the eggs. Stir the eggs with a fork in a circular motion. When the eggs start to set and form curds, spread them out evenly across the bottom of the pan. Immediately turn the heat to very low.

Wait a few more seconds and, when the top layer of egg is almost entirely set, sprinkle the cheese over the surface. Dot the surface with the pesto. Scatter the tomatoes and a handful of the croutons over half of the omelet and fold the other half over the filled side. Slide the omelet out of the pan and serve at once. Serve with home fries or at dinner with a small serving of seafood.

Tomato, Cheddar, and Mushroom Breakfast Squares

Courtesy of the National Dairy Council
www.nationaldairycouncil.org

Ingredients:

2 teaspoons butter

2 cups sliced mushrooms

½ cup sliced green onion, including green tops

4 medium tomatoes

6 slices thick bread, cubed

2 cups shredded, reduced-fat cheddar cheese

2 cups fat-free low-fat milk

2 cups egg substitute

1 teaspoon hot pepper sauce

¼ teaspoon salt

Make ahead suggestion:
After assembling the recipe and covering with foil, you can refrigerate the ingredients for 8–10 hours before baking.

Directions:

Preheat oven to 350°F. Spray an 8- x 8-inch square glass or ceramic baking dish with

cooking spray; set aside. In a medium skillet over medium heat, melt the butter and add the mushrooms. Cook about 5 minutes or until mushrooms are softened and brown at the edges. Stir in green onion and tomatoes; set aside. Place half of the bread cubes in the prepared baking dish. Scatter half of the mushroom mixture and half of the cheese over the bread cubes. Layer the remaining bread cubes and mushroom mixture; set aside.

In a large bowl, beat the milk, egg substitute, pepper sauce, and salt until well

blended. Pour the milk mixture over the bread cubes and top with the remaining cheese.

Cover the dish with foil and bake for 45 minutes. Remove foil and bake for an additional

15 minutes or until top is puffed up and cheese is browned at the edges. Let cool for 5 minutes, and then cut into squares to serve.

Breakfast Burritos

Courtesy of Monica Musetti-Carlin, as seen in
Country Comfort: Holidays

Ingredients:

1 package soft tortillas
1 dozen scrambled eggs
3 tablespoons butter, to coat tortillas and scramble eggs
1 green pepper, finely chopped
Grape tomatoes, finely diced
Scallions, green stems only, finely chopped
2 cups cheddar cheese, shredded
1 tablespoon each fresh parsley and/or cilantro, finely chopped

Guacamole

3 ripe avocados
1 tablespoon mayonnaise
Juice of ½ lemon
1 large stalk celery, finely diced
½ clove pressed garlic
1 tablespoon fresh cilantro, finely chopped

Salsa

3 cups fresh-diced cherry or grape tomatoes
Juice of 1 small lime
2 cloves of garlic, finely diced
1 purple onion, finely chopped
1 ripe mango, 1 unripe mango, both skinned and diced
½ cup roasted poblano peppers, finely chopped
2 tablespoons fresh cilantro, finely chopped

Directions:

Keep the tortillas covered and warm in the oven until ready to roll your burrito. Microwave pepper for 2 minutes, and set aside. Scramble the eggs. Butter a tortilla and fill with one portion of egg, green pepper, tomatoes, scallion, and cheese. Sprinkle with parsley and cilantro, if desired, and roll, making a pocket on the bottom to hold in the ingredients. Serve alone or with an assortment of "choose your own" sides: guacamole, salsa, sour cream, pickled jalapeños, and black beans.

Guacamole

Mash avocados and mix in the ingredients as written in the order above. Serve chilled.

Salsa

Mix all the ingredients. Chill and serve.

"Leftovers" Frittata Bake

Courtesy of Christine Gable, Queen of the Quick Meal
(www.quickmealhelp.com)

Serves 4

Ingredients:

2 tablespoons vegetable oil
1 medium onion, minced
3 cups leftover vegetables
1 cup diced or crushed tomatoes, with juice
1 teaspoon oregano
1 teaspoon basil
¼ teaspoon garlic salt
¼ teaspoon pepper
6 eggs, lightly beaten
½ cup cheese, shredded

Directions:

Preheat oven to 375°F. Spray a 9- x13-inch casserole dish with vegetable oil spray. Set aside. Add oil to heavy skillet over medium heat; add onion and sauté for 1 to 2 minutes. Add vegetables, tomatoes, herbs, garlic salt, and pepper. Sauté for 3 to 4 minutes.

Spread vegetable mixture in bottom of oiled casserole dish and pour eggs on top. Sprinkle cheese on top. Bake for 22 to 24 minutes until golden brown.

Mexican Melt

Courtesy of Monica Musetti-Carlin, as seen in
Country Comfort: Casserole Cooking
Serves 6

Ingredients:

¾ pound pork sausage
6 cups cubed bread
1½ cups cheddar and Monterey Jack cheese, shredded
4 eggs
¾ cup milk
1 cup salsa
Salt, to taste

Directions:

Sauté sausage until browned thoroughly. Drain off excess fat in paper towel. Using an 11- x 7- x 2-inch casserole dish, put in the sausage, and top with the bread and cheeses. Whisk the eggs and milk, mix with salsa, and pour over the sausage and bread to fully coat. Refrigerate overnight. Preheat oven to 350°F and cook, uncovered, for 45 minutes or until firm.

Summer Medley Quiche

Courtesy of Red Fire Farm

(www.redfirefarm.com)

Ingredients:

2 tablespoons olive oil or butter
2½ cups sautéed vegetables (onion, summer squash/zucchini,
pepper, kale, and fresh herbs such as savory or sage)
2 cloves garlic, minced
1 pie shell
½ cup grated cheese of your choice
5 eggs
1 cup whole milk or cream
1 sprig basil, chopped
1 tomato, sliced
½ teaspoon salt and pepper

Directions:

In a large frying pan, sauté the vegetables with the olive oil or
butter. Start with the onions and then add the summer squash/
zucchini, pepper, fresh herbs, kale, and add the garlic last. When
all the vegetables are tender, drain off any liquid and spread
them out on the bottom of the crust. Sprinkle the cheese over
the top.

Wisk the eggs with the milk and add ½ teaspoon salt and pepper and pour over the vegetables. Top with the basil and tomato
and bake at 375°F until puffed and brown (about 30 minutes).
Enjoy hot or cold.

Cheese and Spinach Strudel with Warm Tomato Relish

Courtesy of the Florida Tomato Committee
www.floridatomatoes.org
Serves 6

Ingredients:
Strudel

1 (10 oz.) package frozen chopped spinach
½ pound ricotta cheese
1 cup grated mozzarella cheese
⅔ cup freshly grated Parmesan cheese
2 pinches ground nutmeg
6 sheets phyllo dough, measuring 14- x 18-inches each
3 tablespoons unsalted butter
Fine dry bread crumbs
Salt and freshly ground pepper, to taste

Warm Tomato Relish

2 tablespoons olive oil
1 small onion, minced
1 celery rib, minced
4 large tomatoes, cored, seeded, and coarsely chopped
½ cup grated carrot
1 teaspoon fresh thyme or ½ teaspoon dried
1 teaspoon fresh lemon juice
2 teaspoons chopped fresh parsley
Salt and freshly ground pepper, to taste

Directions:
Strudel

Cook the spinach according to the package directions and cool on a plate. Squeeze out the excess moisture by hand and mix with the cheeses in a bowl. Stir in the nutmeg, salt, and pepper to taste. Preheat the oven to 375°F. To assemble, lay a sheet of phyllo on your work surface with a short edge facing you. Brush it lightly with butter and sprinkle with crumbs. Repeat this, layering until all the sheets of phyllo are used. About 3 inches from the short edge facing you, arrange the filling in a mounded row, about 3 inches wide, leaving about 3 inches uncovered along each long edge so that you can fold the sides over. Fold the sides of the phyllo over the filling and then fold the short end of exposed phyllo over the filling. Continue to roll the phyllo into a log. Poke two small steam vents in the top with a paring knife. Place the strudel on a baking sheet and bake for 30 to 40 minutes, until golden brown.

Warm Tomato Relish

While the strudel bakes, make the relish. Heat the oil in a medium-size nonreactive saucepan. Stir in the onion and celery and sauté over medium heat for 3 minutes. Stir in the tomatoes, carrot, thyme, and salt and pepper to taste. Simmer the relish gently until most of the liquid has cooked off. Remove from the heat. Right before serving, reheat the relish. Remove from heat and stir in the lemon juice and parsley. Slice the strudel and serve hot with some of the relish spooned around each slice.

Breakfast Tomatoes

Courtesy of Mariquita Farm

(www.mariquita.com)

Ingredients:

6 tomatoes, halved

Diced garlic, to taste

Olive oil, to taste

Salt and freshly ground pepper, to taste

Directions:

Sprinkle tomatoes with garlic and olive oil. Broil under the broiler until they are pleasantly browned. Season with salt and pepper to your liking. Serve with eggs or toast.

These are a great way to get a vegetable serving into your first meal of the day.

Baked Eggs in Tomato Cups

Courtesy of Greensgrow Farm
(www.greensgrow.org)

Ingredients:

4 large tomatoes
1 cup grated Parmesan cheese, or less to taste
4 eggs
1 tablespoon fresh herbs such as oregano, basil, or sage
Salt and freshly ground pepper, to taste

Directions:

Preheat oven to 425°F. Slice tops off tomatoes, then scoop out
seeds and pulp. Place tomatoes in a shallow baking dish and
sprinkle cavities with salt, pepper, and a few pinches of cheese.
Crack one egg into each tomato. Sprinkle with salt, pepper,
herbs, and remaining cheese. Bake for 20 minutes for soft yolks
or 30 to 35 minutes for hard yolks. Serve immediately.

Soups & Salads

Cabbage Soup
Courtesy of Audrey Roberts

Ingredients:
1 head cabbage, chopped
1 medium onion, chopped
2 large apples, cut in pieces
1 large can tomatoes, chopped
1 large bone or 1½ pounds soup meat
1 can tomato soup
2 cups water
1 tablespoon flour
Salt, pepper, lemon juice, and sugar to taste

Directions:
Cook the cabbage, onion, apples, and bone (or soup meat) together for 1 hour. Add one can of tomato soup and water, then cook for 45 minutes on a low flame. Stir occasionally to keep from sticking to the pot. Take approximately ½ cup of the liquid from the soup and thoroughly mix in 1 tablespoon of flour. Pour back into the soup pot and stir until it thickens. Add the salt and pepper plus the lemon juice and sugar to taste.

Tomato Basil Soup

Courtesy of Mary Kay Ratigan and Tom Bresnahan

Serves 4

Ingredients:

1 large red onion, chopped
1 tablespoon butter
1 tablespoon ginger, minced
1 tablespoon brown sugar
4 cups whole Roma or plum tomatoes, diced
5 cups chicken stock
1 cup basil leaves
Salt and freshly cracked pepper, to taste

Directions:

In a large saucepan, caramelize the onions in butter, ginger, and sugar. Add the tomatoes and bring to a simmer. Season with salt and pepper

Add the stock and simmer on low heat until very soft (at least 20 minutes). Add the basil and puree.

Cook on low heat for 40 minutes.

How to Peel a Tomato

An easy way to loosen the skins from tomatoes is to blanch them. To do this, core a few tomatoes, and then place them in a pot of boiling water until the skins start to split. Immediately remove them from the water and place them in a bowl of iced water. With a sharp knife, start on the top edge and begin to peel.

Beef Stew

Courtesy of Amy Pawliw

Serves 6–8

Ingredients:

1-inch cubes beef stew meat
1 onion, chopped
1–2 cloves garlic, minced
3–4 cups water
2–3 beef bouillon cubes
8 carrots, sliced
6 stalks of celery, diced
4 cups plum tomatoes, skinned and diced
¾ cup red wine
3–4 potatoes, cubed
1½ cups fresh peas
Salt and pepper, to taste

Directions:

Brown beef in olive oil. Add onion and garlic and brown well.
Add water, bouillon, chopped carrots, celery, tomatoes, wine, salt,
and pepper. Add potatoes, and simmer for 1 hour. Add peas and
more salt, pepper, and wine to taste.

If needed to thicken, add a corn starch slurry.

Vegetable Soup

Ingredients:

2 quarts (8–10 cups) chicken broth
3 cups mixed vegetables (pumpkin, string beans, celery, green peas, turnips, summer squash, onions, asparagus)
Parsnip, cabbage, potatoes (optional)
1 tomato, diced
1 cup water
1 tablespoon corn starch
Salt and pepper, to taste

Directions:

Bring the chicken broth to a boil over medium heat and then cut all vegetables into small cubes. Boil any hard vegetables (such as carrots, pumpkin, turnips, onions, string beans, and celery) before adding them to the pot. Strain the vegetables and place them in the boiling broth. Add any softer vegetables (like cauliflower, asparagus heads, and peas) directly into the broth. Lastly, add the tomato. Dissolve one tablespoon of corn starch in a cup of water and pour in soup. Season soup to taste and stir often. Allow the soup to cook until all ingredients are well-cooked.

Deluxe Cream of Tomato Soup

Courtesy of the Florida Tomato Committee
(www.floridatomatoes.org)
Serves 4–6

Ingredients:
2 tablespoons unsalted butter
1 small onion, finely chopped
2 celery ribs, finely chopped
4 large tomatoes, peeled, cored, seeded, and chopped (see note)
1 teaspoon sugar
2 cups chicken broth
½ cup heavy cream
2 teaspoons chopped fresh dill weed or 1 teaspoon dried
Salt and freshly ground pepper, to taste

Directions:
Melt the butter in a medium-size nonreactive saucepan. Add the onion and celery and sauté gently over medium heat for 5 minutes, stirring often; do not brown. Stir in the tomatoes and sugar. Simmer, covered, for 6 to 8 minutes, until the tomatoes are soft.

Transfer the vegetables to a food processor and process to a smooth puree. Pour the puree back into the saucepan and stir in the remaining ingredients. Heat the soup through, adjusting the seasoning as desired. Serve hot. Round it out with grilled cheese sandwiches, potato chips, and pickles, and you've got the makings for a surefire family favorite.

To peel the tomatoes, submerge them for 15 to 30 seconds in boiling water. Remove to a colander and rinse briefly under cold water. The skins will slip right off.

Roasted Tomato Soup

Courtesy of the Central New York Tomatofest, from the kitchen
of Nadine Vande Walker
(www.cnytomatofest.org)
Serves 5–6

Ingredients:
6–7 medium tomatoes
½ medium red onion
3 tablespoons olive oil
2 teaspoons kosher salt
1 teaspoon sugar
1 teaspoon ground pepper
1 (14½ oz.) can chicken stock
1 cup light cream
2 tablespoons sugar
1 tablespoon fresh sliced basil
Salt, to taste
Sour cream, to garnish (optional)

Directions:
Preheat oven to 425°F. Cut tomatoes into quarters and spread
out on a cookie sheet with the onions. Drizzle with oil. Sprinkle
salt, sugar, and pepper on top. Roast the tomatoes for 30-40
minutes until the tomatoes and onions are tender and a little
brown around the edges. Pour the tomatoes, onions, and juices
into a saucepan. Add chicken stock, light cream, sugar, basil,
and additional salt to the tomato mixture. Simmer for 30 minutes. Use a hand blender to puree until smooth. Serve with a
little dollop of sour cream (optional).

Fire-Roasted Tomato Gumbo
Courtesy of the Florida Tomato Committee
(www.floridatomatoes.org)
Serves 6

Ingredients:

5 large fully ripened fresh tomatoes (about 2½ pounds)
2 tablespoons butter
½ cup coarsely chopped andouille sausage
½ cup coarsely chopped onion
¼ cup coarsely chopped carrot
⅓ cup coarsely chopped celery
2 teaspoons finely chopped garlic
3 tablespoons all-purpose flour
3 cups chicken stock
3 tablespoons tomato paste

2 teaspoons sugar
1 teaspoon chopped fresh rosemary
½ teaspoon salt
¼–½ teaspoon ground red pepper (cayenne), optional
¼ teaspoon ground white pepper
1 cup cooked white rice
¼ cup heavy cream
Croutons and rosemary sprigs, for garnish (optional)

Directions:

Set a grill or broiler rack about 4 inches from the heat source; preheat the grill or broiler. Core the tomatoes and place on the grill or in the roasting pan under the broiler. Cook, turning once, until the skin blackens (30 to 40 minutes).

In a medium saucepan, melt the butter; add the sausage, onion, carrot, celery, and garlic. Cook, stirring occasionally, until the vegetables just begin to brown (about 5 minutes); reduce heat to low. Sprinkle flour over the vegetables; cook and stir until flour begins to brown (3 to 5 minutes).

In a blender or food processor, coarsely chop the grilled tomatoes; add the tomatoes to the vegetables in the saucepan. Stir in the stock, tomato paste, sugar, rosemary, salt, red pepper, and white pepper. Simmer, partially covered, for 15 minutes.

Add rice and cream, then cook just until hot. Spoon into soup plates dividing equally. Garnish with croutons and rosemary sprigs, if desired.

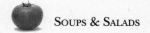

Pepper and Tomato Stew

Courtesy of the Central New York Tomatofest, from the kitchen of Jason G. Wittwer
(www.cnytomatofest.org)

Ingredients:

1 green pepper, chopped
1 red pepper, chopped
1 medium white onion, diced
2 large tomatoes, diced and chopped
2 cups stewed tomatoes
1 pound lean ground turkey
1 pound ground Italian sausage (mild)
1 teaspoon Frank's® Red Hot sauce
1 teaspoon garlic powder
Salt and pepper, to taste
Fresh basil, to garnish

Directions:

Sauté the green pepper, red pepper, and onion in a medium pan over medium heat. Set aside in a 2-quart saucepan. Add the chopped tomatoes and stewed tomatoes. In a skillet, brown the ground turkey. When the turkey is browned, add to the saucepan.

In the same skillet, brown the sausage. When the sausage is browned, add it to the saucepan. Place saucepan over low heat and simmer for 30 minutes or more.

Add the hot sauce, garlic powder, salt, and pepper.

Serve in a bowl. Garnish with fresh basil. Serve with garlic bread or crackers.

A crock pot may be used in place of the 2-quart saucepan.

Gazpacho

Ingredients:

3 large tomatoes, quartered
2 cups cucumber, chopped
1 cup onion, chopped
1 cup green bell pepper, seeded and chopped
2 tablespoon red wine vinegar
2 teaspoons olive oil
1 clove garlic, chopped
1 cup water
Salt and freshly ground pepper, to taste

Directions:

Place tomatoes, cucumber, onion, bell pepper, vinegar, oil, and garlic in a food processor and process until desired consistency is reached. Place vegetable mixture in a serving bowl, add water, and stir thoroughly. Cover and refrigerate for at least 1 hour. Add salt and pepper to taste.

Black Bean Gazpacho

Ingredients:

2 large tomatoes, seeded and chopped
1 large red bell pepper, chopped
1 large green bell pepper, chopped
1 medium cucumber, peeled and chopped
2 celery stalks, thinly sliced
¼ cup sliced green onions
3 cups no-salt-added tomato juice

2 tablespoons lime juice
2 tablespoons red wine vinegar
2 teaspoons Tabasco sauce
½ teaspoon low-sodium Worcestershire sauce
1 garlic clove, minced
2 (15 oz.) cans low-sodium black beans, rinsed and drained
¼ cup fat-free sour cream

Directions:

Mix all ingredients (except sour cream) in a large bowl. Cover and refrigerate for at least 6 hours, stirring occasionally. Serve with sour cream.

Tomato and Asparagus Salad
Courtesy of the British Tomato Growers' Association
(www.britishtomatoes.co.uk)
Serves 4

Ingredients:
4 ounces asparagus tips
8 ounces vine ripened tomatoes, thickly sliced
1 ounce pine kernels, toasted
2 tablespoons hot horseradish sauce
4 tablespoons garlic wine vinegar
8 tablespoons extra-virgin olive oil
Crisp salad leaves

Directions:
Cook the asparagus in water for 4 to 5 minutes. Drain, rinse
under cold water, and then drain again. Place asparagus, tomatoes, and pine kernels in a bowl. Whisk remaining ingredients
together, then pour over tomatoes and toss together. Arrange
salad leaves on plates, then spoon on tomato and asparagus.

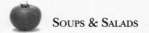

Marinated Goat Cheese and Tomato Salad

Courtesy of the Florida Tomato Committee
(www.floridatomatoes.org)

Serves 4

Ingredients:

½ cup olive oil
½ teaspoon crushed fennel seed (see note)
½ teaspoon dried basil or several fresh basil leaves, torn into piece
1¼ pound (4 oz.) log goat cheese
1 head Boston lettuce, separated into leaves

2 large tomatoes, cut into wedges
3 tablespoons fresh lemon juice
1½ tablespoons honey
¼ cup toasted chopped pecans or walnuts (optional)
Salt and freshly ground pepper, to taste

Directions:

Blend the oil, fennel seed, basil, and pepper in a pottery bowl or pie plate. Slice the goat cheese into eight rounds and lay them in the oil. Cover and marinate at room temperature for 2 to 3 hours.

When you are ready to serve the salad, arrange the salad greens on individual serving plates. Place several tomato wedges and two rounds of goat cheese on each plate, reserving the marinade. Sprinkle with toasted pecans or walnuts.

Heat the lemon juice and honey in a small skillet just long enough to liquefy the honey. Whisk the lemon and honey and a pinch or two of salt into the reserved marinade and serve some of this dressing over each salad.

Marinating goat cheese in olive oil, basil, and crushed fennel seeds softens the flavor of the cheese and makes it taste especially wonderful with the tomatoes. The marinade is mixed with lemon juice and honey, then used as a vinaigrette dressing with the salad. A few toasted nuts scattered on top of each salad are a nice touch.

To crush whole fennel seed, use a rolling pin.

Tomato-Avocado Salad
with Mango-Citrus Vinaigrette

Courtesy of the Ciruli Brothers
(www.champagnemango.com)

Serves 4

Ingredients:

Mango-Citrus Vinaigrette

1 orange (juice and zest)
2 Champagne® mangos, peeled
and seeded
¼ cup red wine vinegar
1 teaspoon honey
1 teaspoon soy sauce
¼ teaspoon Dijon mustard
½ cup canola oil
Salt and freshly ground
pepper, to taste

Salad

1 (10 oz.) package mixed
greens or spring mix
1 medium avocado, peeled and
sliced
2 large Roma tomatoes, cut
into wedges

Directions:

Mango-Citrus Vinaigrette

In a blender, puree all vinaigrette ingredients (except the oil) on
the lowest setting. Slowly drizzle in the oil until it is completely
incorporated. Salt and pepper to taste.

Salad

Combine greens, avocado, and tomato in a salad bowl, then mix
well. Serve salad on a plate and add just enough of the vinaigrette to coat the greens.

Tuna, Tomato, and Bean Salad

Ingredients:

Dressing
½ teaspoon grated lemon peel
⅓ cup lemon juice
¼ cup olive oil
2 tablespoon fresh chopped parsley
1 teaspoon rosemary
1 tablespoon Dijon mustard

Salad
3 medium green bell peppers
3 medium red bell peppers
2 (15 oz.) cans white beans, rinsed and drained
2 (6 oz.) cans water packed tuna, drained
½ cup sliced ripe olives
1 head lettuce
2 medium tomatoes, cut into wedges

Directions:

Dressing

Mix all dressing ingredients thoroughly in a tightly covered container.

Salad

Set oven to broil. Place the bell peppers on the broiler pan. Broil with the tops 4 to 5 inches from the heat for about 10 minutes on each side or until the skin blisters and browns. Remove from oven. Wrap in towel; let stand for 5 minutes. Remove skin, stems, seeds, and membranes of the peppers. Cut peppers into ¼-inch slices. Toss peppers, beans, tuna, olives, and dressing in a bowl. Cover and chill for 4 hours, stirring occasionally. Spoon salad onto lettuce leaves and garnish with tomato wedges.

Moroccan Lentil and Tomato Salad

Ingredients:

1¼ cups uncooked lentils
2½ cups water
3 tablespoons lemon juice
1½ tablespoons olive oil
½ teaspoon thyme
½ teaspoon mint flakes
¼ teaspoon salt
⅛ teaspoon black pepper
1 garlic clove
1½ cups quartered cherry tomatoes
1 cup diced cucumber
1½ cups crumbled reduced-fat feta cheese
1 cup thinly sliced celery
4 cups romaine lettuce leaves

Directions:

Place lentils and water in a large saucepan; bring to a boil.
Cover, reduce heat, and simmer for 20 minutes or until tender.
Drain well and set aside. Combine lemon juice, olive oil, thyme,
mint, salt, pepper, and garlic in a medium bowl; stir with a wire
whisk until blended. Add lentils, tomatoes, cucumber, cheese, and
celery to dressing mixture; toss gently to coat. Serve on plates
lined with romaine lettuce.

Cold Pasta Salad with Char-Grilled Tomato Sauce

Courtesy of the British Tomato Growers' Association
(www.britishtomatoes.co.uk)

Serves 4

Ingredients:

2 pounds tomatoes, halved
2 red peppers, halved and de-seeded
2 teaspoons olive oil or cooking spray
Bunch of fresh basil, chopped
6 ounces farfalle tonde pasta
Salt and freshly ground pepper, to taste

Directions:

Pre-heat a grill. Put the halved tomatoes, cut-side facing up-wards, on the grill and grill until charred. Remove from grill and cool. Put peppers on the grill, skin-side facing upwards, and brush with oil. Grill until charred, turn over peppers, and grill the other side until charred and the peppers are soft. Cool peppers in a plastic bag. Scrape the cooled tomatoes from their skins and put into a bowl. Skin the cooled peppers and cut into small pieces. Mix with the tomatoes. Stir in the chopped basil and season to taste. Cook pasta according to package instructions, making sure it is 'al dente'. Strain pasta and plunge into cold water to cool. When cool, drain thoroughly. Mix pasta with prepared tomato and pepper sauce. Serve with a baby spinach salad.

Fish & Seafood Entrées

Chilean Sea Bass
with Black Bean Salsa

Courtesy of Monica Musetti-Carlin, as seen in
Country Comfort: Holidays

Ingredients:

4 pounds Chilean sea bass fillets

1 can black beans, drained

1 each red, green, and yellow pepper, diced

1 small red onion, finely chopped

2 cups cherry tomatoes, quartered

1 small avocado, diced

1 cup mango, diced

⅛ cup balsamic vinegar

¹⁄₁₆ cup extra-virgin olive oil

1 cup fresh cilantro, finely chopped

2 tablespoons garlic powder

1 tablespoon cumin

1½ tablespoons chili powder

1 teaspoon Spanish paprika

Juice of 1 lime

Salt, to taste

Directions:

Sprinkle the sea bass with garlic powder, cumin, chili powder, and paprika, and bake at 350°F for 45 minutes.

Combine the black beans, peppers, onion, tomatoes, avocado, mango, balsamic vinegar, olive oil, cilantro, and the remaining spices. Let it sit for about 1 hour.

Squeeze the juice of 1 lime over the sea bass when it comes out of the oven, and then spoon on the black bean salsa and serve.

Crawfish Louise

Courtesy of Chef Joe Fein, The Court of Two Sisters
(www.courtoftwosisters.com)
Serves 2

Ingredients:

1 pound crawfish (or shrimp) tails and fat
1 tablespoon butter
3 tablespoons olive oil
1 bunch green onions, diced ¼-inch thick
½ pound large mushrooms, julienne-cut ¼-inch thick
1 tablespoon garlic, pureed
1 medium tomato, diced ¼-inch thick
½ cup Italian-flavored breadcrumbs
½ cup Parmesan cheese
Salt and black pepper, to taste

Directions:

Heat crawfish tails and fat, and set aside. Melt butter and oil, and then sauté green onions, mushrooms, and garlic. Add tomato, crawfish, breadcrumbs, and Parmesan cheese. Place in a casserole dish, and heat thoroughly in a 350°F oven for 30 minutes. Add salt and pepper to taste, if desired.

Fire-Roasted Mussels with Fresh Tomato Salsa

Courtesy of Chef Christopher Holt, George Martin: The Original
(www.georgemartingroup.com)

Serves 4

Ingredients:

Mussels

3 pounds farm-raised mussels
(preferably Prince Edward
Island), cleaned with beards
removed
3 tablespoons olive oil
1 teaspoon kosher salt
¼ teaspoon freshly cracked
black pepper

Fresh Tomato Salsa

3 medium ripe tomatoes,
chopped
½ small red onion, chopped
6 leaves cilantro, chopped
Juice of 1 lime
2 teaspoons red wine vinegar
6 teaspoons olive oil
Dash of Tabasco or hot sauce
Sea salt and freshly cracked
black pepper, to taste

Directions:

Mussels

Discard any mussels that are open or have broken shells. Gently toss the mussels with the olive oil, salt, and pepper. Chill the mussels until ready to grill.

On a hot, clean grill, gently place the mussels, and cover with the grill lid (if your grill does not have a lid, cover the mussels with a large metal bowl).

Cook for 2 minutes, and as the mussels pop open, remove them from the grill and place in a large bowl, so, you can toss them with your choice of sauce.

Fresh Tomato Salsa

Chop the tomatoes, red onion, and cilantro by hand or simply pulse in your food processor. Add the lime, vinegar, oil, hot sauce, salt, and pepper. Stir well and let it rest for 1 hour before adding to your mussels. Serve this version of the mussels with a clean, crisp pilsner beer.

Mussels with Tomato Wine Sauce

Courtesy of the Florida Tomato Committee

(www.floridatomatoes.org)

Serves 5

Ingredients:

2 pounds mussels
¼ cup water
1 tablespoon unsalted butter
1 small onion, minced
1 clove garlic, minced
4 large tomatoes, cored, seeded, and coarsely chopped
¾ cup dry white wine
1 tablespoon minced fresh parsley
Salt and freshly ground pepper, to taste

Directions:

Scrub the mussels under cold running water, pulling off the "beards" with your hands. Put the water in a large pot, add the mussels, cover, and place on a burner with the heat turned off.

Mussels over pasta or rice make an inexpensive appetizer or main course. Here they are served as a main course, so you may want to double the sauce so you have extra for the pasta.

Melt the butter in a medium-sized saucepan. Add the onion and sauté, stirring over medium heat for 2 minutes. Stir in the garlic, sauté for 30 seconds, then add the tomatoes. Turn the burner under the mussels to high.

Cook the tomatoes for 2 minutes, then add the wine and season to taste. Quickly bring the tomatoes to a boil and boil for about 5 to 8 minutes, until the sauce is as thick as you like. Stir in the parsley and keep the sauce over very low heat.

Meanwhile, steam the mussels for about 6 to 8 minutes, until they've opened. Discard any that don't open. Arrange the mussels on serving plates. Spread the shells slightly, or break off the empty half, and spoon some of the sauce over each mussel. Serve immediately.

Linguini with Little Neck Clams and Vegetables

Courtesy of Chef Joseph DeNicola, La Tavola Restaurant

(www.latavolasayville.com)

Ingredients:

24 Little Neck clams

1 pound linguini

2 medium zucchini, cut into half-moons

2 medium yellow squash, cut into half-moons

8 ounces pancetta

2 tablespoons garlic

4 ounces fresh basil, sliced

15 red and yellow cherry tomatoes, halved

1 cup lemon juice

2 cups white wine

4 ounces extra-virgin olive oil

½ cup clam broth

Directions:

Sauté pancetta in olive oil until crispy. Add garlic and vegetables and sauté until golden brown. Add lemon juice, white wine, and clam broth.

Bring to a boil. Add clams. Let them steam until they open. Add fresh basil.

In a separate pot, boil linguini in salted water. Strain the pasta and place in a serving bowl.

Arrange clams, vegetables, and sauce on top of pasta.

Curried Conch, Mango, and Tomato Chowder

Courtesy of the Ciruli Brothers
(www.champagnemango.com)

Serves 4

Ingredients:

1 tablespoon olive oil
1 carrot, diced
1 stick celery, diced
1 onion, diced
1 ear corn, roasted and
cut off the cob
1 pound conch meat, sliced
very thin (you may substitute
with shrimp)
2 slightly green Champagne®
mangos, diced
2 tablespoons yellow curry
paste

2 tomatoes, chopped
1 stalk lemongrass, cut into
1-inch strips and lightly
crushed with the flat of a knife
1 cup chicken stock or water
1 (14 oz.) can coconut milk
1 teaspoon chopped chives
1 teaspoon chopped cilantro

Directions:

In a medium saucepan, combine oil, carrot, celery, onion, and corn. Sauté for 30 seconds, then add the conch. Sauté for an additional 30 seconds then add the diced mango and curry paste. Cook for an additional 30 seconds and then add the tomatoes, lemongrass, chicken stock, and coconut milk. Simmer for 4–5 minutes on low. Add the herbs and serve

Shrimp and Tilapia Ceviche

Courtesy of the Ciruli Brothers
(www.champagnemango.com)
Serves 16

Ingredients:

16 large shrimp, peeled, de-veined, and diced
1½ pounds tilapia, diced
3 Champagne® mangos, peeled and diced
1 cucumber, peeled and diced
3 large Roma tomatoes, finely diced
¼ yellow onion, finely diced
Juice of 6 limes
½ cup clamato juice (picante)

Directions:

Mix all ingredients in a bowl and cover with plastic wrap so that all the fish and shrimp are submerged under the liquid. Refrigerate for at least 5 hours before serving. Best served with fried tortilla chips.

In traditional ceviche recipes (such as this one) the shrimp is not cooked, but instead is cured in the lemon juice until it turns pink.

Fresh Corn, Tomato, and Scallop Pasta

Courtesy of the National Pasta Association

(www.Ilovepasta.org)

Serves 6

Ingredients:

1 pound medium shells, ziti, or other medium pasta shape, uncooked

1 tablespoon plus 1 teaspoon olive or vegetable oil

¾ cup sliced red onion

1 pound bay scallops or medium shrimp, peeled and deveined

1 cup fresh or frozen corn kernels (2 ears)

2 cloves garlic, minced

4 large ripe tomatoes, peeled, seeded, and diced (about 4 cups)

2 tablespoons minced fresh oregano

½ teaspoon dried rosemary

½–1 teaspoon hot sauce

2 tablespoons red wine vinegar

1 tablespoon e lemon juice

½ cup crumbled feta cheese

Salt and freshly ground pepper, to taste

Directions:

Prepare pasta according to package directions. While pasta is cooking, heat 1 tablespoon oil in a large skillet. Add red onion and cook for about 2 minutes. Add scallops, corn, and garlic. Cook for 4 minutes, stirring often. Add tomatoes, oregano, rosemary, and hot sauce. Simmer just until scallops are done and mixture is thoroughly heated, about 5 minutes. Stir in red wine vinegar and lemon juice.

When pasta is done, drain well. Transfer to a serving bowl. Drizzle with remaining 1 teaspoon oil and toss well. Spoon tomato mixture over pasta. Sprinkle with cheese, salt, and pepper. Serve immediately.

Rotini with Tuna and Tomato

Courtesy of the National Pasta Association
(www.Ilovepasta.org)

Serves 6

Ingredients:

8 ounces rotini, twists, or spirals, uncooked
1 (6⅛ oz.) can solid white tuna, packed in water, drained
1 medium zucchini, diced
1 green bell pepper, ribs and seeds removed, diced
1 medium tomato, peeled, seeded, and chopped
3 scallions, sliced
¼ cup drained capers (optional)
2 tablespoons vegetable or olive oil
2 tablespoons lemon juice
1 teaspoon minced fresh basil
2 tablespoons minced fresh parsley
Freshly ground pepper, to taste

Directions:

Cook pasta according to package directions; drain and chill.
Combine pasta, tuna, zucchini, bell pepper, tomato, scallions, and
capers; toss. Mix remaining ingredients and pour over the pasta
mixture. Toss lightly and serve.

Crispy Angel Hair Cakes with Scallops, Escarole, and Tomato Coulis

Courtesy of the National Pasta Association

(www.Ilovepasta.org)

Serves 4

Ingredients:

8 ounces angel hair pasta
6 plum tomatoes, quartered
5 cloves garlic, peeled and coarsely chopped
4 teaspoons olive oil, divided
8 sea scallops
4 ounces pancetta, diced

1 large shallot, minced
1 small head escarole, washed, trimmed, and chopped
4 basil sprigs, for garnishing
Salt and freshly ground black pepper, to taste

Directions:

Preheat the oven to 450°F.

Cook the pasta according to package directions. Rinse, drain, and set aside.

On a baking sheet with sides, toss together the tomatoes, garlic, 1 teaspoon olive oil, and salt and pepper. Roast the tomatoes until they are very soft, about 20 minutes. Remove the tomatoes and reduce the oven temperature to 375°F. While the tomatoes are roasting, make the pasta cakes. Warm 1 teaspoon olive oil in a small, non-stick sauté pan over medium-high heat. Add a generous ½ cup of pasta to the pan and flatten it into a pancake shape. Fry on both sides until golden brown. Transfer to a baking sheet. Make three more cakes in the same way and then four small, lacy cakes to use as tops. Set the cakes aside until needed.

When the tomatoes are ready, puree them in a blender or food processor until smooth. Strain into a saucepan, cover, and set over very low heat until needed.

Warm 1 teaspoon olive oil in a medium, non-stick sauté pan over very high heat. Add the scallops and brown them on both sides, about 1 minute per side. Do not overcook the scallops. Transfer to a small baking sheet and set aside until needed. Reduce the heat under the sauté pan to medium and add the last teaspoon of olive oil. Sauté the pancetta and shallots for 3 or 4 minutes. Add the escarole and cook until wilted. Season with salt and pepper to taste.

While the escarole is wilting, put the pasta cakes and scallops in the oven to warm.

To assemble, spoon some tomato coulis onto each of four plates. Set a large pasta cake on the coulis. Top each with ¼ of the escarole. Slice the scallops in half crosswise and set four slices on each mound of escarole. Finish with a small pasta cake set in place at an angle. Garnish with basil and serve immediately.

Shrimp Creole

Courtesy of Mary Carlin, as seen in
Country Comfort: Casserole Cooking
Serves 4

Ingredients:

1 onion, chopped
1 cup chopped green pepper
2 cloves garlic
¼ cup extra-virgin olive oil
2 teaspoons sea salt
½ teaspoon pepper
½ teaspoon chili powder

2 cups raw shrimp, shelled and
deveined
2 cups rice, cooked
2 (8 oz.) cans tomato sauce
1 (15½ oz.) can whole tomatoes
1 cup water

Directions:

Add onion, green pepper, and garlic to heated oil, and cook for
10 minutes over medium to low heat. Add seasonings, cook
another 2 minutes, transfer to a bowl, and mix with shrimp.
Line the bottom of your casserole dish with cooked rice. Mix the
shrimp mixture with the tomato sauce, tomatoes, and water;
then pour over rice. Bake at 350°F for 30 minutes or until liquid is mostly absorbed. Let sit for 5 minutes before serving.

Mexican Shrimp Cocktail

Courtesy of A Silverware Affaire

(www.asilverwareaffair.net)

Serves 2

Ingredients:

Shrimp

10 large gulf shrimp, peeled
and deveined
1 tablespoon extra-virgin
olive oil
1 teaspoon garlic salt
Juice from ½ lime
Freshly cracked black pepper,
to taste

Cocktail Sauce

1 avocado, diced
½ red onion, diced
1 whole red tomato, diced
1 whole jalapeño, diced
¼ red bell pepper, diced
¼ cup fresh cilantro, chopped
¼ cup kernel corn
Juice of ½ lime
8 ounces organic tortilla chips
Sea salt and freshly cracked
black pepper, to taste

Directions:

Shrimp

Sauté shrimp in olive oil with garlic salt, pepper, and lime until
pink and cooked through (approximately 5 minutes).

Cocktail Sauce

Mix the above ingredients lightly and place in martini glasses.
Garnish with shrimp and tortilla chips.

Grilled Southwestern Shrimp

Courtesy of the Florida Tomato Committee
(www.floridatomatoes.org)
Serves 4–6

Ingredients:

4 large tomatoes
2 tablespoons olive oil or vegetable oil
2–3 tablespoons canned chipotle peppers, chopped
2 tablespoons chopped pickled jalapeño peppers
¼ cup tomato juice

2 tablespoons fresh lime juice
1 tablespoon packed light brown sugar
¼ teaspoon salt
2 tablespoons minced fresh parsley
3 tablespoons minced red onion
1 pound (16–20) large shrimp, peeled and deveined

Directions:

Core, halve, and seed two tomatoes. Chop them coarsely and transfer to a bowl. Core the remaining two tomatoes, then cut each horizontally into three thick slices. Rub one surface of each slice with a little of the oil. Grill over hot coals for 8 to 10 minutes, oiled side down, until quite soft.

In the bowl of a food processor, combine the grilled tomatoes, chipotle peppers, jalapeño peppers, tomato juice, lime juice, brown sugar, and salt. Process to a slightly rough puree, then stir the puree into the chopped fresh tomatoes. Stir in the parsley and onion. Set aside while you grill the shrimp.

Toss the shrimp with the remaining oil in a bowl. Thread the shrimp onto skewers, salt and pepper them lightly, then grill over hot coals for 3 to 4 minutes on each side or until opaque throughout. Serve hot with plenty of the sauce on the side.

If you can take the heat, try these big grilled shrimp with blazing tomato salsa. You'll find the canned chipotle peppers (the source of the heat) in most well-stocked supermarkets or in specialty food stores.

Pasta with Tomatoes, Shrimp, and Feta

Courtesy of the Florida Tomato Committee
(www.floridatomatoes.org)
Serves 4–6

Ingredients:

1 cup olive oil
4 green onions, finely chopped
1 green bell pepper, seeded and finely chopped
1 teaspoon hot pepper flakes
1 tablespoon fresh (or 1 teaspoon dried) oregano, finely chopped
½ cup Italian parsley, finely chopped
1 pound medium shrimp, peeled and deveined
4 medium firm, ripe tomatoes, peeled, seeded and chopped
1 tablespoon tomato paste
½ cup white wine
1 pound penne pasta
½ pound feta cheese, crumbled
Salt and freshly ground pepper, to taste

Directions:

Warm oil in a large skillet over medium heat. Add green onions and cook, stirring constantly, until transparent (about 5 minutes). Add bell peppers, hot pepper flakes, oregano, and parsley. Salt and pepper to taste and cook, stirring constantly, until peppers are soft.

Reduce heat to medium-low. Add shrimp and cook until they are no longer pink. Add the tomatoes and cook until they release their juices. Add tomato paste and white wine and cook for about 20 minutes. Set aside and keep warm in the oven.

Bring 5 quarts of water to a boil. Add pasta and 1 teaspoon salt. Stir and cook until firm to the bite, about 8 to 10 minutes.

Drain the pasta and toss with the sauce. Sprinkle feta cheese over top. Serve immediately.

This very sophisticated and light pasta dish is delightful with crusty bread and a light green salad for a very special summertime meal.

Lime Shrimp and Tomato Kebobs

Serves 2

Ingredients:

3 large limes
2 cloves garlic, crushed and peeled
¼ teaspoon black pepper
2 teaspoons olive oil
2 tablespoons fresh cilantro, cleaned and chopped
16 large shrimp, uncooked and deveined

10 medium cherry tomatoes, rinsed and dried
10 small white-button mushrooms, wiped clean and stems removed

Directions:

In a glass measuring cup, squeeze limes, yielding ¼ cup of juice. Add the garlic, pepper, olive oil, and cilantro and stir. Place the shrimp in a medium bowl and pour the cilantro lime marinade over the shrimp. Let the shrimp marinate for 10 to 15 minutes in the refrigerator (do not let them marinate for more than 30 minutes as the acid of the juice will alter the texture of the shrimp). Alternate cherry tomatoes, mushrooms, and shrimp on four skewers. Grill the skewers over medium heat for 3 to 4 minutes on each side until the shrimp are just cooked through.

Fish and Tomato Thai Curry

Courtesy of the British Tomato Growers' Association

(www.britishtomatoes.co.uk)

Serves 6

Ingredients:

Curry Sauce

3 shallots, finely chopped

2 cloves garlic, finely chopped

2 bird's eye chilies, seeds removed and finely chopped

3 kaffir lime leaves

2 inches galangal (or ginger), scraped and cut into 4 pieces

2 sticks lemongrass, trimmed and cut lengthways

1 bunch coriander, chopped

1 teaspoon green Thai curry paste

1 ¼ teaspoons shrimp paste

1 cup reduced-fat coconut milk

1 cup semi-skimmed milk

Fish

1 pound, 2 ounces plum tomatoes

1 ½ pounds firm white fish (such as monkfish or Antarctic icefish)

1 ¼ cups Thai fragrant rice

Directions:

Curry Sauce

Prepare the ingredients for the curry sauce. Put them all into a saucepan and bring slowly to a boil, stirring constantly. Cover and simmer for 5 minutes. Cool, then remove lime leaves, galangal (or ginger), and lemongrass with a slotted spoon and discard. Pour sauce into a blender and pulse until smooth.

Fish

Skin and quarter the tomatoes. Cut fish into 1-inch cubes. Cook rice according to package instructions. Put tomatoes and fish into a large saucepan. Pour the sauce over the fish and tomatoes. Bring slowly to a boil and simmer for 6 minutes or until fish is cooked. Serve on rice.

Try finding Thai curry packs in the fresh produce section of your supermarket—they contain most of the ingredients required for the sauce.

Spanish Paella with Tomatoes

Serves 4

Ingredients:

2 tablespoons olive oil
1 medium onion, diced
1 clove garlic, minced
1 cup rice, dry
1 cup diced red pepper
¾ cup diced zucchini
2½ cups low-sodium chicken broth
¾ cup frozen peas, thawed
1¾ cups tomatoes, chopped

1 (15 oz.) can chickpeas, rinsed and drained
1 pound peeled shrimp
⅛ teaspoon salt
⅛ teaspoon pepper
⅛ teaspoon saffron

Directions:

Heat olive oil in oven-safe large skillet. Add onion and garlic. Stir for 3 minutes on medium heat.

Add rice, red pepper, zucchini, and ½ cup of chicken broth. Stir for another 5 minutes. Add remaining ingredients, except shrimp. Stir and place skillet in the oven. Bake at 375°F for 20 minutes. Add shrimp. Cook until shrimp turns pink, about 5 minutes.

Meat & Poultry Entrées

Lasagna

Courtesy of Kathleen Gallagher

Ingredients:

1½ boxes lasagna noodles
3 quarts of your favorite tomato sauce, divided
1½ pounds lean ground beef
4 cups mozzarella cheese, shredded
2 cups Parmigiano-Reggiano cheese, grated and divided
3 pounds ricotta cheese
1 (16 oz.) ounce bag fresh baby spinach, washed and drained
3 eggs
3 sprigs fresh parsley, finely chopped
1 tablespoon dried oregano
3–4 tablespoons extra-virgin olive oil, divided
Salt and freshly cracked pepper, to taste

Directions:

Preheat an oven to 350°F.

Prepare in Advance

Combine the ricotta cheese with 1 cup of grated cheese, three eggs, spinach, parsley, oregano, salt, and pepper. Mix and refrigerate.

Meat Sauce

Brown, season with salt and pepper, and drain the ground beef. Combine with 2 quarts of sauce and simmer for about ½ hour.

Noodles

Cook the lasagna noodles according to the package directions, adding 3 tablespoons of olive oil to the water. Keep the cooked lasagna noodles in cool water while layering.

Assembling the Lasagna

Coat a deep-dish pan (2½-inches deep; approximately 10- x 8-inches long and wide) with the remaining oil. Spoon a layer of the remaining sauce into the bottom of the pan. Place a layer of cooked lasagna noodles across the pan, slightly overlapping the edges. Spoon on a layer of meat sauce. Next, spoon on about 8 tablespoons of ricotta cheese mixture. Generously sprinkle with grated cheese, and then the mozzarella cheese. Cover with another layer of noodles, repeating the layers of the meat sauce, ricotta mixture, grated cheese, and mozzarella. Cover with the last layer of noodles, spooning on more meat sauce. Decoratively arrange tablespoons of ricotta-cheese mixture and mozzarella to cover the top. Sprinkle with grated cheese, and bake loosely covered in the preheated oven for approximately 1½ hours or until bubbling nicely.

Lasagna Mexicana

Courtesy of Gretel Carlin

Serves 8-12

Ingredients:

1 pound ground sirloin
½ cup yellow onion, chopped
1 (1¼ oz.) envelope Old El Paso® Taco Seasoning Mix
1 (8 oz.) can tomato sauce
1 (15 oz.) can Old El Paso® Mexi-Beans
1 (4 oz.) can green chilies, chopped
6 (8 in.) flour tortillas, halved; divided
2 cups cheddar cheese, shredded and divided

Directions:

Brown beef and onion in skillet. Drain. Stir in seasoning. Mix in tomato sauce, Mexi-Beans, and green chilies. Layer half of tortillas on bottom of a 12- x 8-inch casserole dish. Spread half of meat mixture and then sprinkle half of cheese over tortillas.

Repeat layers. Bake in a preheated, 350°F oven. Let stand 10 minutes before serving.

Turkey Nachos

Courtesy of Monica Musetti-Carlin, as seen
in *Country Comfort: Holidays*

Ingredients:

1½ cups taco chips
1 cup sliced black olives
1 cup black beans
½ yellow onion, finely diced
2 tomatoes, diced
½ cup cilantro, chopped
½ each red and green peppers, finely diced
1½ cups shredded cheddar and Monterey Jack cheeses
Shredded leftover turkey, as needed

Directions:

Spread the taco chips in a baking dish, and layer the ingredients
as they appear above. Microwave on high until the cheese is fully
melted (about 2–6 minutes) or bake in the oven for about 20–25
minutes (or until cheese is melted). Serve with sour cream and
guacamole.

Chicken Cacciatore

Courtesy of Ann Del Vecchio McNulty

Ingredients:

6 tablespoons extra-virgin olive oil
3 pounds chicken fryer, cut up
1 cup onion, minced
1 cup green pepper, sliced
4 cloves garlic, minced
2 (8 oz.) cans tomato sauce
2½ cups diced tomatoes
½ cup Chianti wine
¾ teaspoons allspice
2 bay leaves
½ teaspoon dried thyme
Dash cayenne pepper

Directions:

Sauté the chicken in olive oil until golden brown. Add the onion, green pepper, and garlic, and brown lightly. Add the wine. Add the remaining ingredients, and bring to a simmer. Continue to simmer, uncovered, for 30 minutes to 1 hour.

Best Chicken Salad Stuffed Tomato Crowns

Courtesy of the Florida Tomato Committee
(www.floridatomatoes.org)

Serves 4

Ingredients:

4 medium fresh tomatoes
½ cup plain low-fat yogurt
2 cups chicken, cooked, shredded, and chilled
¼ cup flat-leaf parsley, chopped
½ cup celery, small diced
½ cup carrots, small diced
1 lemon, juiced
1 small onion, small diced
Kosher salt and freshly ground pepper, to taste

Directions:

Rinse tomatoes under cold running water and pat dry with clean paper towels. With a sharp serrated knife, slice off the top part of the tomato that was attached to the vine. Turn the tomato over and make four to five slices almost all the way down, but be careful not to slice all the way through the tomato. Set tomatoes aside.

In a medium-sized mixing bowl, combine all ingredients except the tomatoes. Taste the chicken salad and adjust seasoning with the kosher salt and freshly ground pepper. Using a fork, separate the sliced tomatoes open and fill with chicken salad. Serve chilled.

Pan-Roasted Chicken with Heirloom Tomatoes and Fresh Bay Leaf

Courtesy of Mariquita Farm

(www.mariquita.com)

Ingredients:

2 boneless chicken breasts (about 6 ounces each), skin-on
2 fresh bay leaves
2 teaspoons grapeseed oil
4–6 cloves roasted garlic
2 cups reduced chicken stock
1 purple Cherokee tomato, sliced ½-inch thick
1 big daddy sunshine tomato, sliced ½-inch thick
2–3 small green zebra tomatoes, sliced ½-inch thick
6 yellow pear tomatoes, slit in half lengthwise
6 red pear tomatoes, slit in half lengthwise
Sea salt and freshly ground pepper, to taste
6 year aged balsamic vinegar, to taste

Directions:

Insert a fresh bay leaf between the skin and meat of each chicken breast. Cover and

refrigerate for one hour. Remove the bay leaves and reserve. Heat a medium sauté pan over a low flame (see note) for several minutes until the pan is quite hot. Lightly season each chicken breast with salt and pepper on both sides. Rub the grapeseed oil onto the skin of each chicken breast and place the breasts, skin side down, into the hot sauté pan. Turn the heat up to medium and allow the breasts to cook until well browned. Turn the chicken breasts over, and then use a paper towel to absorb the excess fat.

Add the roasted garlic and allow to heat until they become fragrant. Add the chicken stock and simmer for 3 to 5 minutes, depending on the thickness of the chicken breasts. Remove the breasts to a heated holding plate and keep warm.

Increase the flame and reduce the chicken stock until it coats a spoon like syrup.

Reduce the flame and add the tomatoes. Allow the tomatoes to just heat through. Swirl the pan (rather than stirring) so the tomatoes retain their individual shape and color. Remove from the flame immediately and swirl in the reserved bay leaves. Season to taste with salt and pepper. Add balsamic vinegar if the sauce needs acidity. Divide the tomato sauce to the centers of two warmed bowls or deep-rimmed plates. Place the chicken breasts over the sauce, garnish with the bay leaves, and serve with toasted crusty bread.

This method of preparation uses a low temperature sauté. Leaving the pan over a low flame for a long period of time allows the pan to get hot enough to put a good sear on the chicken. Turning the fire up once the chicken is added gently brings the heat of the pan back to a point which allows the skin to crisp without scorching.

Roasted Chicken Legs with Jalapeño and Tomato

Courtesy of Greensgrow Farm

(www.greensgrow.org)

Serves 2

Ingredients:

1 tablespoon olive oil

2 teaspoons fresh lime juice

2 whole chicken legs (about 1 pound total)

2 small tomatoes, cut into ½-inch slices

2 jalapeño chilies, seeded (if desired) and cut into ¼-inch slices

1 small onion, cut into ¼-inch slices

1 garlic clove, sliced thin

½ cup low-sodium chicken broth

Salt and freshly ground pepper, to taste

Directions:

Preheat oven to 450°F.

In a bowl, stir together the oil and lime juice. Add the chicken legs and toss to coat. Arrange the chicken legs, skin side facing upwards, in a roasting pan and season with salt and pepper. Add tomatoes, chilies, onion, garlic, and salt to the oil mixture and toss well. Spread the vegetable mixture around the chicken legs in one layer and roast for 30 minutes on the upper rack of an oven, until chicken is cooked through.

Transfer chicken to a platter and keep warm, covered with foil. Add broth to the vegetables in the pan and boil over medium-high heat, scraping up browned bits until sauce thickens slightly, about 2 to 3 minutes. Serve chicken with sauce and vegetables.

Spaghetti Pie

Courtesy of Michele Melara

Serves 8-12

Ingredients:

½ pound spaghetti or vermicelli, cooked
2 large eggs (brown or white), beaten
¾ cup Romano cheese, grated
1 (10-inch) pie pan
1 pound lean ground beef or turkey/chicken/lamb
½ cup celery, diced
½ cup sweet onion, finely diced
1 (4 oz.) can mushrooms, drained
1 cup stewed tomatoes, drained
1½ cups spaghetti sauce
5 slices mozzarella cheese

Directions:

Combine cooked spaghetti with beaten eggs and grated cheese. The mixture should then be placed into a 9-inch round, shallow casserole dish, and pressed evenly. Combine browned ground meat (or turkey, beef, chicken, or lamb) with celery, onion, mushrooms, tomatoes, and spaghetti sauce, and let simmer for 15 minutes. Then pour mixture over spaghetti and cover evenly.

After everything looks even and tasty, cover with foil and bake at 350°F for 25 to 30 minutes. After 30 minutes has passed, take pie out of the oven and then top with the five mozzarella cheese slices. The cheese will not be fully melted so place back in the oven for another 3 to 5 minutes or until the cheese is melted.

Osso Buco Milanese

Courtesy of Chef Keith Brunell, Maggiano's "Little Italy"
(www.maggianos.com)

Ingredients:

6 ounces olive oil

6 (12–14 oz.) veal shanks

⅔ cup all-purpose flour

1 large carrot, peeled and cut into ¾-inch pieces

1 yellow onion, peeled and cut into ¾-inch pieces

2 ribs celery, cut into ¾-inch pieces

3 tablespoons fresh garlic, chopped

12 ounces white wine

6 ounces orange juice

1 quart veal stock or beef broth (low-sodium)

1 quart chicken stock (low-sodium)

1 (38 oz.) can crushed tomatoes (San Marzano or plum)

1 sprig fresh rosemary, finely chopped

2 sprigs fresh thyme, finely chopped

4 tablespoons salt-pepper mix

2 teaspoons fresh lemon zest, to garnish

1 tablespoon fresh parsley, finely chopped, to garnish

Directions:

Heat the olive oil in a casserole dish. Dredge all sides of the veal shanks with all-purpose flour, place into the dish, and brown on all sides for about 4 to 5 minutes per side until a deep golden brown is formed. Remove from the dish and place onto a plate or tray to rest.

Add the carrots, onions, and celery, then cooking for approximately 4 to 5 minutes. Add the chopped garlic and cook for another minute until slightly roasted.

Add the remaining flour and cook for 3 minutes to form a roux or a slight paste. Then add white wine and reduce until almost dry.

Add the orange juice, beef broth (or veal stock), chicken stock, crushed tomatoes, rosemary, thyme, salt, and pepper, and simmer slowly for another 4 to 5 minutes. Add the veal shanks back to the vegetables and sauce.

Place a lid or aluminum foil onto the dish and cook at 275°F for approximately 2 to 2½ hours or until fork-tender, being careful not to overcook.

Once cooked, use a metal spatula to carefully remove from the oven and transfer each individual osso bucco to the serving dish.

Then place in the same oven to dry out for about 10 minutes (this allows the muscle to contract and caramelize on the outside). Remove from the oven. Remove any excess fat or oil from sauce, and bring to a simmer while the veal is drying out.

Pour the thickened sauce over all veal. Garnish with fresh lemon zest and chopped parsley. Serve with risotto, creamy or crispy polenta, or mashed potatoes.

Moussaka

Courtesy of Chef Stavros Kokkosis, Aegean Café

(www.sayvilleaegeancafe.com)

Serves 6

Ingredients:

3 large eggplants
1 pound potatoes
1 large yellow onion, finely chopped
1 pound ground lamb or beef
1 pound tomatoes, peeled and diced
¾ teaspoon sugar, divided
½ teaspoon cinnamon
1 bunch flat-leaf parsley, finely chopped
4 tablespoons butter
½ cup all-purpose flour
3 cups milk
1 egg yolk
½ teaspoon nutmeg, freshly grated
2 teaspoons lemon juice
Graviera cheese, grated, for topping
¾ cup breadcrumbs
Extra-virgin olive oil, as needed
Salt and pepper, to taste

Directions:

Wash the eggplants. Remove the base of the stalk and cut lengthwise in three (8-inch) slices. Place the slices in a bowl, cover with water, sprinkle with salt, and leave to dry for 20 minutes. Meantime, peel the potatoes, cut into three (8-inch) slices, and add salt.

Drain the eggplant and pat dry. Heat the olive oil in a pan and brown the eggplant on both sides over high heat (you will have to keep adding oil as they cook). Remove the slices from the pan and place on paper towels to drain. Put fresh olive oil in the pan, fry, and drain the potato slices in the same way. Sauté the onion until transparent, add the ground meat, and brown over high heat.

Stir in the tomatoes, ¼ teaspoon of sugar, ½ teaspoon cinnamon, and one bunch of parsley, and then reduce heat and simmer for 10 minutes. Prepare the béchamel sauce by melting the butter in a pan, and then stir in the flour and cook for a minute or two, slowly pouring in the milk while stirring continuously. When the mixture thickens, remove the pan from the heat, stir in the egg yolk, and season the sauce with the remaining ½ teaspoon of sugar, ½ teaspoon of nutmeg, 2 teaspoons of lemon juice, and salt and pepper to taste. Stir in 2 tablespoons of the grated Graviera and allow to cool.

Preheat oven to 350°F. Cover the base of a large casserole dish first with a layer of potato slices, and then half the ground meat mixture. Next, layer the eggplant slices, and then the remaining ground meat. Pour over the béchamel sauce, smooth over the top, and sprinkle with breadcrumbs, cheese, and additional cinnamon (if desired). Cook for about 45 to 60 minutes until the top is golden brown. Allow the finished dish to cool a little before cutting into large portions for serving. Serve with freshly baked white bread.

Chili

Courtesy of Dorothy Acierno
Serves 12

Ingredients:

5 pounds beef brisket, chuck or any inexpensive cut of meat
1 large yellow onion, sliced
Vegetable oil for browning meat
3 tablespoons chili powder
1 tablespoon cayenne pepper flakes
2 (28 oz.) cans tomato puree
28 ounces water
1 (12 oz.) can, kidney beans
1 (8–12 oz.) jar sliced jalapeño peppers (optional)
1 pound cheddar cheese, shredded (optional)
Salt and freshly ground pepper, to taste

Directions:

Brown the meat on all sides in the vegetable oil, add the onion, cover, and cook as you would for a pot roast (at least 3 hours), until the meat is falling apart. Then shred the meat and add in the remaining ingredients in the order written above, except the jalapeños and cheese. Cook for about 1–1½ hours, stirring occasionally. If you desire a thinner consistency, add a little water; to make it a bit thicker, add a little tomato paste. Serve with jalapeño peppers and cheese on the side (optional).

Grilled Flat Iron Steaks with Sun-Dried Tomato Chimichurri

Courtesy of Chef Sonali Ruder

Serves 4

Ingredients:

¼ cup extra-virgin olive oil
¼ cup sun-dried tomatoes, packed in oil, finely chopped
2 tablespoons oil from the jar of sun-dried tomatoes
4 cloves garlic, sliced very thin
3 tablespoons balsamic vinegar

¼ cup fresh parsley, chopped
4 (8 oz.) shoulder top-blade (flat iron) steaks, cut 1-inch thick
Kosher salt and freshly cracked black pepper, to taste

Directions:

Preheat a gas or charcoal grill over medium-high heat. Heat the olive oil, sun-dried tomatoes, 2 tablespoons of sun-dried tomato oil, and garlic in a medium frying pan over medium heat for

3–4 minutes, until the flavors are infused into the oil. Pour the mixture into a medium bowl and stir in the balsamic vinegar, parsley, salt, and pepper. Set aside.

Season the steaks generously with salt and pepper on both sides. Grill the steaks, covered, for 11–14 minutes for medium-rare to medium doneness, turning occasionally. Let the meat rest, and then slice across the grain. Arrange slices on a platter topped with the sun-dried tomato chimichurri.

Baked Fresh Tomato, Ham, and Swiss Rolls

Courtesy of the Florida Tomato Committee
(www.floridatomatoes.org)

Serves 4

Ingredients:

2 large fresh tomatoes (about 1 pound)
6 ounces sliced ham, cut in strips (about 1½ cups)
6 ounces Swiss cheese, shredded (1½ cups)
3 tablespoons creamy mustard blend
1 tablespoon prepared white horseradish
4 large, hard round (Kaiser) rolls, cut in halves

Directions:

Use tomatoes held at room temperature until fully ripe. Core tomatoes, cut in large chunks, and set aside. Preheat oven to 400°F. In a medium bowl combine the ham, cheese, mustard blend, and horseradish. Gently stir in the tomatoes. Remove the inside from the bottom portion of each roll, leaving ½- to ¾-inch thick shells. Place on a baking sheet. Fill each shell with about 1 cup of the tomato mixture and top with the upper portion of the roll. Bake until heated through and cheese starts to melt, about 15 minutes.

Stuffed Pork Tenderloin with Fresh Tomato Sauce

Courtesy of Carrie Balkcom, American Grassfed Association
(www.americangrassfed.org)

Serves 6–8

Ingredients:

Fresh Tomato Sauce

1¾ pounds Roma tomatoes (see note)
1 teaspoon olive oil
½ cup onion, diced
1 clove garlic, minced
½ cup tomato paste
2 cups chicken or vegetable stock (or more as needed)
2 tablespoons fresh basil, chopped
Salt and freshly ground black pepper, to taste

Pork

2 pork loins (about 4 pounds), trimmed
1 (4 oz.) log fresh goat cheese
3 tablespoons fresh rosemary, minced
2 tablespoons minced garlic
½ teaspoon salt
½ teaspoon freshly ground pepper
1 tablespoon olive oil
Rosemary sprigs, for garnish
Salt and freshly ground pepper, to taste

Directions:

Fresh Tomato Sauce

Peel, seed, and chop tomatoes. In large sauté pan that can be fitted with a lid, heat oil. Adjust temperature to medium heat, then add onions and garlic. Cover and sweat until soft, about 5 to 7 minutes. Add tomatoes and tomato paste and pincé over medium heat until rust-colored (see note). Add 1 cup of stock, stir, and cover pan. Simmer, stirring occasionally until sauce is thick, about 45 minutes (if sauce appears too thick during cooking time, add a little more stock to obtain desired consistency). Add basil and season with salt and pepper.

Pork

While Tomato Sauce is cooking, prepare pork loins. Preheat oven to 400°F. Cut each pork loin in half lengthwise, but not through one edge. Open the tenderloin like a book and spread half of the goat cheese along the inside of each loin. Season with salt and pepper.

With a mortar and pestle, make a coarse paste of the minced rosemary, garlic, salt, and pepper. Spread over all sides of both pork loins. Tie loins with unwaxed string and allow to stand at room temperature for 30 minutes.

Heat large oven-proof sauté pan over medium-high heat. Add olive oil and heat. Sear pork loins on all sides and transfer pan to preheated oven. Roast for 15 minutes for medium doneness. Remove from then oven and cover pan with foil. Allow meat to rest for 5 minutes before slicing. Slice loins about ½-inch thick and serve with Fresh Tomato Sauce strewn across the slices. Garnish with a few rosemary sprigs.

If tomatoes are out of season, you can improve the flavor by roasting them if desired. Cut the tomatoes in half lengthwise, seed them, and place them cut-side up on a baking sheet. Roast in a 325°F oven for about 30 minutes. Remove skins and continue with the recipe.

Allowing tomato paste to pincé or "cook out" reduces the raw flavor (excessive sweetness, bitterness, or acidity) in the tomato paste. Tomato paste cooks out very quickly on the stovetop. Be careful not to burn.

Pasta with Tomato Meat Sauce
Courtesy of the National Pasta Association
(www.Ilovepasta.com)
Serves 4–6

Ingredients:

1 pound pasta, uncooked
8 ounces lean ground beef
1 medium onion, chopped
2 cloves garlic, minced
6 large tomatoes, peeled, seeded, and diced
½–1 teaspoon salt

½ teaspoon dried oregano
½ teaspoon dried basil
½ teaspoon sugar
¼ cup red wine

Directions:

Prepare pasta according to package directions.

While pasta is cooking, combine beef, onion, and garlic in a large skillet; cook until meat is no longer pink. Set aside. In blender, combine remaining ingredients; process for 30 seconds. Add tomato mixture to meat; simmer about 20 minutes.

When pasta is done, drain well. Add the sauce to the pasta and serve.

Vegetarian Entrées

Eggplant Parmigiana

Courtesy of Betty Meyers

Serves 4-6

Ingredients:

1 large eggplant
2 cups flour
2 eggs
2 tablespoons milk (optional)
½ cup corn or vegetable oil
4 cups Italian tomato sauce
1 cup grated Parmesan cheese
4 ounces mozzarella cheese, sliced
Salt and pepper, to taste

Directions:

Peel eggplant and cut into ¼-inch-round slices. Soak in cold, salted water for about 15 minutes, draining thoroughly. In large bowl, combine flour, salt, and pepper. In small bowl, beat eggs and add small amount of milk, if necessary. Coat eggplant slices well on both sides with flour. In 12-inch skillet, heat oil. Meantime, dip floured eggplant in eggs on both sides and transfer onto flat plate. When oil is ready (when pinch of flour dropped in oil bubbles), cook slices (about four or five at a time) until golden brown on each side, turning once. Remove to paper towel-lined pan. Repeat with remaining slices, adding oil if necessary.

When ready to bake, line bottom of casserole dish with layer of sauce, a layer of eggplant slices, and a layer of grated Parmesan cheese sprinkled liberally over the slices. Then repeat: sauce, eggplant, and Parmesan for three more layers. Place mozzarella slices on top layer. In preheated oven, cover dish lightly with foil and bake at 375°F for about 30 minutes. Remove cover and bake another 15 minutes. Let stand for at least 15 minutes after removing from oven before serving.

Vegetarian Chili

Courtesy of Monica Musetti-Carlin, as seen in
Country Comfort: Harvest

Ingredients:

4 teaspoons chili powder
1 large onion, sliced
3 garlic cloves, crushed
1½ cups diced plum tomatoes,
or 1 large can crushed tomatoes
1 large can black beans, drained
1 cup each corn and carrots
2 cups tempeh, crumbled
1 cup raw nuts (pistachios or
cashews)

3 cups water
Cilantro or sour cream, to
garnish
Extra-virgin olive oil, as needed

Directions:

Sauté the onion and garlic in olive oil. Add the chopped nuts and chili powder. Add the tomatoes, water, and beans, and cook for 1 hour. Add the corn and carrots, and after 10 minutes, add the crumbled tempeh. Salt and pepper to taste. Add the garnish.

Mediterranean Wrap

Courtesy of Susan Prior

Serves 4

Ingredients:

¾ cup tomato, chopped

1 tablespoon purple onion, diced

1 tablespoon fresh cilantro, chopped

1 teaspoon lime juice

⅛ teaspoon sea salt

1 clove garlic, minced

1 cup long-grain rice, cooked

2 teaspoons basil

1 cup sweet red pepper, chopped

¾ cup zucchini, diced

¾ cup yellow squash, diced

¼ cup purple onion, diced

2 tablespoons balsamic vinegar

2 teaspoons olive oil

4 (8-inch) tortillas

¼ cup feta cheese, crumbled

Directions:

Combine first six ingredients in a bowl; set tomato mixture aside.

Combine rice and basil; set aside.

Arrange sweet red pepper, zucchini, yellow squash, and onion in a single layer on a baking sheet. Broil for 12 minutes or until vegetables are browned, then spoon into a large bowl. Drizzle vinegar and olive oil over vegetables, and toss to coat.

Warm tortillas according to package directions. Spoon ¼ cup of the rice mixture down the center of each tortilla. Top each serving with ½ cup of the roasted vegetables, 2 tablespoons of the tomato mixture, and 1 tablespoon of feta cheese; roll up.

Hot Stuffed Tomatoes

Courtesy of the British Tomato Growers' Association

(www.britishtomatoes.co.uk)

Serves 4

Ingredients:

4 British Beef tomatoes
1 ounce margarine
1 medium onion, peeled and finely chopped
1 small clove garlic, peeled and crushed
2 sticks celery, finely chopped
1½ ounces fresh whole-wheat breadcrumbs
1 tablespoon chopped fresh herbs (such as basil, oregano, and marjoram)

Directions:

Stand the tomatoes on their stem ends and slice off the tops. Remove the pulp with a small spoon and set aside. Stand tomatoes upside down to drain. Melt the margarine in a pan and fry the onion, garlic, and celery until soft but not browned. Stir in the breadcrumbs, herbs, and tomato pulp. Season well. Fill the tomato cases with the mixture and replace the tops. Cook in the oven at 350°F for about 20 minutes. Serve hot.

Spaghetti Squash with Fresh Tomato Sauce

Courtesy of Red Fire Farm

(www.redfirefarm.com)

Ingredients:

1 large spaghetti squash

2 onions, chopped

2 cloves garlic

1 red or green bell pepper, chopped

5 tomatoes, chopped

1 bunch basil

Olive oil

Grated Parmesan cheese, to taste

Salt and freshly ground pepper, to taste

Directions:

Cut squash in half lengthwise and scoop out the seeds. Place face down on a pan with ¼-inch of water and bake for 40 minutes at 350°F.

While baking, start the sauce. In olive oil, sauté onions, garlic, and peppers for 5 minutes on medium heat. Add tomatoes, salt, and pepper to taste and simmer for the remainder of the squash prep time. Remove squash from the oven and stick a fork into the cut side. The fork should go in easily, but it should not be mushy.

Cool for 5 minutes and use the fork to scrape the strands of squash from the skin, trying to keep them intact. Serve immediately topped with the sauce, fresh chopped basil, and cheese.

Eggplant and Tomato Shish Kabobs with Pineapple, Sesame Rice, and Sweet Chili Sauce

Courtesy of www.ILoveEggplant.com

Ingredients:

Skewers

1 Japanese eggplant, stem ends removed, cut into 1-inch wedges
1 yellow squash, cut into 1-inch wedges
1 red bell pepper, cut into 1-inch by 1-inch sections
8 cherry tomatoes per serving
1 red onion, cut into 1-inch by 1-inch sections
8 button mushrooms
Mae Ploy™ Sweet Chili Sauce, for dipping

Rice

1 cup jasmine rice
1 cup water
¾ cup canned pineapple
½ teaspoon curry powder
Salt and freshly ground pepper, to taste

Directions:

Skewers

Stick alternating vegetables on skewers and set aside for grilling.

Rice

Next, place all rice ingredients in a small stockpot and bring to a simmer. Cover and turn the burner down to low heat. Cover the rice and let it cook for 20 minutes. Remove rice from heat, but keep covered until ready to serve.

Grill the kabobs to your desired tenderness. When done grilling, serve the kabobs with the rice and the sweet chili sauce.

If you are using wooden skewers, make sure to soak them in water overnight. This will help prevent them from burning on the grill.

Chickpea, Tomato, and Spinach Curry

Serves 6

Ingredients:

1 cup onion, coarsely chopped

1½ tablespoons fresh ginger, chopped or grated

1 teaspoon olive oil

1½ teaspoons curry powder

1 (19 oz.) can chickpeas, rinsed and drained

1¾ cups tomatoes, chopped

1¼ cups fresh spinach, stems removed

½ cup water

¼ teaspoon salt (optional)

Directions:

Combine onion and ginger in food processor and pulse until minced.

Heat oil in large skillet over medium-high heat. Add onion mixture and curry. Sauté for 3 minutes.

Add chickpeas and tomatoes; simmer for 2 minutes. Stir in spinach, water, and salt. Cook another minute until spinach wilts. Try serving over brown rice.

If you don't have a food processor, chop onion and ginger into small pieces.

Okra with Rice, Tomatoes, and Beans

Ingredients:

½ cup chopped onions
2 cups chopped tomatoes
1 teaspoon sesame oil
1 cup sliced okra
2 cloves garlic, chopped
½ cup low-sodium vegetable broth
2 cups cooked brown rice
1 cup black beans, canned

Directions:

In a medium-sized saucepan, sauté the onions and tomatoes in the oil for 5 minutes. Add the okra, garlic, and broth. Cook for 15 to 20 minutes. Serve hot over the rice and beans.

Fresh Vegetable Pita Pizza

Courtesy of Florida Tomato Committee

(www.floridatomatoes.org)

Serves 4

Ingredients:

1 pound fresh tomatoes

4 (7-inch) pita breads

1 tablespoon olive oil

2 tablespoons grated
Parmesan cheese

1½ teaspoons Italian
seasoning, divided

2 cups shredded part-skim
mozzarella cheese, divided

1 medium zucchini, cut in half
lengthwise and thinly sliced
(2 cups)

1 green pepper, thinly sliced

1 cup thinly sliced sweet red or
white onion

Directions:

Preheat oven to 425°F. Use tomatoes held at room temperature until fully ripe. Core and slice tomatoes; cut each slice in half. Place pitas on two baking sheets; brush with oil. Arrange tomato slices on each pita, dividing evenly. Sprinkle with Parmesan cheese and half of the Italian seasoning. Bake until tomatoes are heated and pitas begin to crisp, about 10 minutes.

Sprinkle tomatoes with half of the mozzarella cheese. Top with zucchini, green pepper, and onion. Sprinkle with remaining mozzarella and Italian seasoning. Bake until cheese is melted and vegetables are crisp-tender, about 10 minutes. Serve with crushed red pepper and additional Parmesan cheese, if desired.

Grilled Eggplant on Potato-Crust Pizza with Basil and Mozzarella

Courtesy of www.ILoveEggplant.com

Serves 4

Ingredients:

Sauce

1 tablespoon olive oil
1 (8 oz.) can whole, peeled tomatoes
1 tablespoon chopped basil
¼ teaspoon dried oregano

Flat Bread

1 russet potato
1 tablespoon olive oil
¼ teaspoon salt
1½ cups flour
1 egg

Topping

1 teaspoon crushed red pepper flakes
1 eggplant, lightly grilled and thinly sliced
4 Roma tomatoes, thinly sliced
1 (8 oz.) ball fresh mozzarella, thinly sliced
5 large basil leaves, roughly chopped
Salt and freshly ground pepper, to taste

Directions:

Sauce

Puree all sauce ingredients and simmer on stove top over medium heat for 10 minutes, then let stand.

Flat Bread

Bake the potato until it is tender, then cool in the refrigerator. Preheat your oven to 500°F. Once the potato is cool, peel it and mash the pulp. Mix in olive oil, salt, flour, and egg and blend well. Let the dough sit at room temperature for 10 minutes to rest. Press dough onto an oiled pizza pan.

Topping

Lightly sprinkle the dough with salt and pepper and add the crushed red pepper. Next, spread sauce on the dough and place an even layer of eggplant, tomatoes, and cheese on top of the dough. Top by sprinkling with chopped basil. Bake the pizza in the oven for approximately 15 minutes or until the crust is golden brown. Cut and serve.

Autumn Vegetable Casserole

Courtesy of Chef Christopher Holt, George Martin: The Original
(www.georgemartingroup.com)

Serves 4

Ingredients:

1 pound dry white beans
(cannelloni or great Northern)

2 tablespoons vegetable oil

1 onion, medium-diced

1 fennel bulb, medium-diced

5 cloves garlic, sliced

10 white mushrooms, sliced

¼ cup white wine

5 cups low-sodium vegetable
stock

10 sun-dried tomatoes, chopped

3 carrots, peeled, split,
and sliced

3 parsnips, peeled, split, and
sliced

4 stalks celery, medium-diced

2 white turnips, medium-diced

2 tablespoons tomato paste

¼ cup tomato sauce

3 sprigs fresh thyme, picked
and chopped

5 sage leaves, chopped

2 sprigs rosemary, picked and
chopped

Salt and pepper, to taste

Crust

1½ cups panko breadcrumbs

¼ cup Pecorino Romano, grated

3 tablespoons olive oil

½ teaspoon parsley, chopped

Salt and pepper, to taste

Finish

White truffle oil (optional)

Directions:

Sort, rinse, and soak white beans overnight in the refrigerator. (You can also use the quick soak method. Sort and rinse the beans and cover with cold water. Bring to a boil, and then remove from heat and cover. Let beans soak for 1 hour; then drain and rinse, again.)

In a large pot (or Dutch oven), add 2 tablespoons of vegetable oil and warm. Add onion, fennel, garlic, and mushrooms to oil, and sauté until translucent. Add wine to deglaze the pan. Add white beans and vegetable stock.

Bring to a boil. Then lower heat to a simmer and allow to cook for 30 minutes.

After the first 30 minutes, add the sun-dried tomatoes, carrots, parsnips, celery, turnips, tomato paste, tomato sauce, and chopped herbs. Continue to simmer another hour, stirring occasionally.

Begin to check the tenderness of the beans (you want them to be tender throughout). Add salt and pepper to taste. Your cooking time will vary, but total cooking time should be 1½ to 2 hours.

Crust

While the beans simmer, prepare your crust. Place breadcrumbs on a cookie sheet in a 350°F oven and toast lightly.

Once toasted, place breadcrumbs in a bowl and add cheese, olive oil, parsley, salt, and pepper. Toss.

Finish

Spoon bean mixture into a large casserole dish (or several smaller casseroles). Top with breadcrumb mixture, return to oven, and bake for 10 to 15 minutes, until bubbly and golden brown. If you are using truffle oil, lightly drizzle the top of the casserole before serving.

Manicotti

Courtesy of Mary Carlin, as seen in
Country Comfort: Casserole Cooking
Serves 6

Ingredients:

1 cup sifted flour
1 cup water
7 eggs, divided
3 tablespoons extra-virgin olive oil
2 pounds ricotta cheese
1 cup grated Parmesan or Romano cheese, grated and divided

¼ teaspoon pepper
½ pound mozzarella, cut into 12 strips
3 (8 oz.) cans tomato sauce (or equivalent in homemade)
Salt, to taste

Directions:

Batter

Combine flour, water, and salt. Beat until smooth. Beat in 4 eggs, one at a time. Heat a 5- to 6-inch skillet and grease with a few drops of olive oil. Put about 3 tablespoons of batter in hot skillet and roll around pan to distribute evenly. Cook over low heat until firm, but not brown. Turn and cook lightly on the other side (no more than 1 minute). Continue making pancakes until all the batter is used (should make 12 to 14 pancakes). Do not re-grease skillet.

Filling

Mix ½ teaspoon of salt, 3 eggs, ricotta, ¼ cup of Parmesan (or Romano) cheese, and pepper. Put about 2 tablespoons of filling and a strip of mozzarella on each pancake and roll up. Pour one can of tomato sauce (or 8 ounces homemade) into a large, shallow casserole dish. Put pancakes seam-side-down in sauce. Cover with the remaining sauce and sprinkle with ½ cup of Parmesan. Bake at 350°F for about 45 minutes. Use the remaining ¼ cup of Parmesan for sprinkling on at the table, if desired.

Spinach Noodle Bake

Courtesy of Diane M. Raab

Serves 6-8

Ingredients:

2 (10½ oz.) packages frozen chopped spinach, thawed and drained

1 pound ziti, cooked and drained

1 pound ricotta cheese

2 (15 oz.) jars marinara sauce

3 eggs, lightly beaten

⅔ cup grated Parmesan cheese

⅓ cup fresh parsley, chopped

2 teaspoons salt

Directions:

Preheat oven to 350°F. Combine all ingredients and mix until well-blended. Put mixture into a lightly greased, 3-quart casserole dish. Bake at 350°F for 30 minutes or until the top is browned and the sauce bubbles.

Ratatouille a la Niçoise

Courtesy of www.ILoveEggplant.com

Serves 5

Ingredients:

6 tablespoons olive oil

1 onion, chopped

1 teaspoon minced garlic

1 large Italian eggplant, stem ends removed and cut in small wedges

1 small yellow squash, stem ends removed and cut in small wedges

1 small zucchini (Italian) squash, stem ends removed and cut in small wedges

2 cups chopped tomatoes

¾ cup of red wine

1 teaspoon of dried Italian seasoning

½ cup black olives

1 cup crumbled feta cheese

Salt and black pepper, to taste

Directions:

In a large skillet, heat about 3 tablespoons of olive oil. Add the onion and garlic, and cook over medium heat until onion is soft. Remove onion and garlic from heat and transfer to a large bowl.

Add the squash and eggplant to pan with remaining oil. Cook until lightly browned on both sides, then add a bit more oil if necessary. When cooked, remove from pan and add to the bowl.

In the skillet, combine the wine, tomatoes and spices. Simmer for approximately 4–5 minutes. Remove from heat, then pour sauce in the bowl, mixing well with the vegetables.

When the mix is slightly cool, add the olives and cheese, mixing well.

Pasta with Tomatoes, Roasted Red Peppers, and Fresh Basil

Courtesy of the Central New York Tomatofest, from the kitchen
of Melissa Gentilcore
(www.cnytomatofest.org)

Ingredients:

2 large red bell peppers
3 tablespoons olive oil
20 fresh medium Roma plum or multi-colored tomatoes
½ teaspoon salt
¼ teaspoon black pepper
1 ½ teaspoons sugar
6–8 medium garlic cloves, coarsely chopped
15 oil-cured olives, pitted and halved
20 fresh basil leaves, torn into pieces
1 pound pasta (rigatoni, shells or ziti)
1 (1 lb.) bag frozen spinach
¼ cup grated Pecorino Romano cheese

Directions:

Line broiler pan or cookie sheet with foil. Rub 2 tablespoons olive oil on red peppers and place them on the pan. Broil, turning frequently until all sides are blackened. Remove from broiler and wrap in aluminum foil. Set aside to cool.

Preheat oven to 425°F.

Cut tomatoes in quarters and place in a 9- x 13-inch baking dish. Sprinkle with salt, pepper, and sugar. Remove skin and seeds from cooled peppers and cut into large strips. Do not discard pepper juice. Add roasted red peppers with juice, chopped garlic, olives, and basil. Drizzle with 1 tablespoon olive oil. Bake for 25 minutes. While tomato mixture is baking, cook pasta and spinach according to package directions. Drain. Mix pasta and spinach together. Put pasta and spinach mixture in large serving dish. Top with baked tomato mixture. Sprinkle with grated cheese.

Summer Tomato Pie

Courtesy of Lisa Rosenberg

Serves 6-8

Ingredients:

Pie Crust

1½ cups all-purpose flour
½ cup plus 1½ tablespoons cornmeal
1½ teaspoons baking powder
½ teaspoon baking soda
½ teaspoon sea salt
6 tablespoons cold, unsalted butter, cut into ½-inch cubes
1 cup buttermilk

Filling

3–4 large ripe red tomatoes, cored and cut into ¼-inch slices
2½ cups (approximately ½ pound) extra-sharp cheddar cheese, coarsely grated
¼ cup Parmigiano Reggiano cheese, finely grated
1 egg
Approximately 2 tablespoons olive oil
¼ cup fresh chives, snipped or chopped
1 tablespoon apple cider vinegar
2 teaspoons sugar
½ teaspoon kosher or sea salt
½ teaspoon black pepper, freshly ground

Directions:

Pie Crust

In a medium-sized bowl, mix the flour, cornmeal, baking powder, baking soda, and salt. Cut in butter with pastry spoon or fingertips until dough resembles coarse meal. Add buttermilk and knead gingerly until ball forms. Wrap dough in plastic and chill for 1 hour.

Filling

Line a baking sheet with several layers of paper towels, and lay sliced tomatoes on top.

Top slices with another several layers of paper towels. Let stand for 30 minutes to drain.

Preheat oven to 425°F. Roll out dough between two sheets of plastic wrap to about a foot around. Remove top layer of plastic and invert into a shallow, 9-inch round, glass casserole dish/pie pan.

Peel off other layer of plastic. Press dough lightly into corners, smoothing down thick spots.

Toss cheeses together in a small bowl until mixed well, reserving ¼ cup of cheese mixture. Beat egg in glass measuring cup and add olive oil to equal ½ cup of total mixture. Add chives, vinegar, sugar, salt, and pepper to that mixture.

Assembly

Sprinkle reserved 1½ tablespoons of cornmeal over bottom of dough in casserole dish. Top with ½ cup of cheese mixture. Arrange one-third of tomato slices over cheese (you can overlap them if needed). Spoon 2 tablespoons of egg mixture over tomatoes. Next, layer 1 cup of cheese mixture, half of remaining tomato slices, and top with rest of egg mixture. Next, layer 1 cup of cheese mixture, then top with remaining tomato slices, and finally sprinkle with reserved ¼ cup of cheese. Trim any extra crust back to level with casserole dish.

Bake pie until crust is golden and cheese is golden brown (about 35–40 minutes). If crust is getting too browned, tent with foil until finished. Do not under-bake. Let pie cool at least 90 minutes before serving.

Tomato and Romano Cheese Pie

Courtesy of Central New York Tomatofest, from the kitchen of
Deborah Oliver
(www.cnytomatofest.org)

Serves 8

Ingredients:

5–6 medium tomatoes,
peeled, sliced, and drained
1 lightly baked 9-inch
pie shell
½–1 cup mayonnaise
½–1 cup grated pecorino
Romano cheese
1 large clove garlic, minced
¼ teaspoon pepper

2 teaspoons dried (or 2
tablespoons fresh) basil
¼ cup Ritz® crackers, crushed
2 teaspoons melted butter
Salt, to taste

Directions:

Preheat oven to 350°F. Arrange tomato slices in pie shell.

Blend all other ingredients except the crackers and butter.

Spread over the sliced tomatoes. Mix cracker crumbs and melted
butter. Sprinkle pie with the cracker/butter mix. Bake for 25-30
minutes.

Fresh Tomato and Cheddar Cheese Pie

Courtesy of the Central New York Tomatofest,
from the kitchen of Lee Parker
(www.cnytomatofest.org)
Serves 8

Ingredients:

9-inch pie crust
5–6 medium tomatoes
1 cup chopped basil
¾ cup mayonnaise
Juice from ½ lemon
1 cup shredded cheddar cheese
½ cup freshly grated Parmesan cheese
¼ cup breadcrumbs
Salt and ground pepper, to taste

Directions:

Preheat oven to 425°F. Line pie plate with crust, prick several
times with fork. Line pie shell with aluminum foil and weight
(dry beans work well). Bake for 5 minutes. Remove from oven
and remove foil and weight. Allow to cool for 15 minutes.

Reduce oven to 400°F. Cut tomatoes into slices approximately
¼ inch thick. Line bottom of pie shell with layer of tomatoes.
Sprinkle with salt, pepper, and chopped fresh basil. Repeat
layers of tomato, salt, pepper, and basil until pie shell is full.
In a small bowl combine mayonnaise with lemon juice, ¾ cup
shredded cheddar cheese, and ¼ cup freshly grated Parmesan
cheese. Spread mayonnaise mixture over surface of tomatoes
and spread to all sides so mayonnaise coats the entire surface
of the crust. Sprinkle with remaining cheddar and Parmesan
cheese. Top with breadcrumbs. Bake at 400°F for 30-40 minutes.
Let cool.

Side Dishes
& Snacks

Sunday Dinner Spaghetti Sauce

Courtesy of Betty Meyers

Ingredients:

1 large onion, chopped

5–6 cloves garlic, sliced

1 (28 oz.) can tomato puree and 1 (28 oz.) can water

6–8 plum tomatoes, skinned and diced, and 1 (28 oz.) can water

1 (6 oz.) can tomato paste and 1 (6 oz.) can water

½ cup fresh oregano, chopped fine, or 2–3 tablespoons dried oregano

Extra-virgin olive oil, as needed

Directions:

In a large sauce pot, cook your onion until translucent, and then the garlic. Add the tomato puree, fresh tomatoes, tomato paste, and water. Sprinkle the oregano over the top and stir.

Place your prepared meatballs in, bring to a boil, and then immediately reduce the heat and cover.

Simmer for 3 hours, stirring from the bottom of the pot to reduce sticking. Skim the top of any excess oil rising to the surface.

Greek Pasta Salad

Courtesy of Darcy Grainger, Darcy's Delights (Sayville, NY)

(www.darcysdelights.com)

Serves 8

Ingredients:
Salad
1 pound bowtie pasta, cooked

2 medium ripe tomatoes, chopped

1 purple onion, sliced fine

4–5 scallions, diced

½ each green, yellow, and red peppers, chopped

½ pound kalamata olives

½–¾ pound feta cheese, crumbled

Dressing
½ teaspoon sea salt (optional)

1–1½ teaspoons freshly cracked black pepper

1–1½ teaspoons garlic powder

1–1½ tablespoons oregano

1 lemon, squeezed thoroughly over salad

¼ cup red wine vinegar

½ cup olive oil

Directions:

In a large salad bowl, toss the ingredients for dressing thoroughly, and pour over feta cheese. Mix in the salad ingredients and serve.

Mozzarella, Tomato, and Red Onion Platter with Basil Drizzle

Courtesy of Mary Elizabeth Roarke, as seen in
Country Comfort: Summer Favorites

Serves 6-8

Ingredients:

Salad Platter

2 large beef-steak tomatoes, thinly sliced

1 (16 oz.) ball fresh mozzarella, thinly sliced

1 large red onion, thinly sliced

Dressing

½ cup good-quality mayonnaise

3 tablespoons white vinegar

2 tablespoons extra-virgin olive oil

2 tablespoons whole milk

1 teaspoon sugar

½ teaspoon sea salt

15 fresh basil leaves

Directions:

Place all the dressing ingredients in a food processor and blend. Assemble the platter by alternately arranging tomatoes, red onions, and mozzarella. Immediately before serving, drizzle sauce over the platter.

Green Tomato Apple Pie

Courtesy of the Central New York Tomatofest, from the kitchen
of Elizabeth Koenig
(www.cnytomatofest.org)

Ingredients:

3 cups sliced green tomatoes
1 large Granny Smith apple,
peeled and diced
1 tablespoon lemon juice
½ cup sugar
½ cup light brown sugar
2 tablespoons flour
1 teaspoon cinnamon

½ teaspoon salt
2 (9-inch) pie crusts
4 tablespoons butter
1 teaspoon sugar

Directions:

Toss tomatoes and apples in a large bowl with lemon juice. Add
sugars, flour, cinnamon, and salt. Mix well. Put one pie crust in
9-inch pie pan. Spread half of the mixture into the pie crust and
dot with 2 tablespoons of butter. Spread the other half of the
mixture on top and dot with of the remaining butter. Cover with
the top crust and crimp the edges with the tines of a fork. Cut
slits in the top of the crust for steam to escape. Bake at 425°F
for 15 minutes, then reduce heat to 350°F and cook for another
45 minutes. In the last 15 minutes of baking time, sprinkle pie
crust with sugar. Cool slightly before serving. Best when served
warm.

Tomato Tart

Courtesy of Central New York Tomatofest, from the kitchen of
Linda Blanding and Maryann Carriagan
(www.cnytomatofest.org)

Ingredients:

Pastry

1¾ cups flour
½ teaspoon salt
1 tablespoon sugar
¾ cup cold unsalted butter, cut
in pieces
4 tablespoons ice water

Filling

¼ cup Dijon mustard
1 pound mozzarella cheese,
thinly sliced
10 medium tomatoes, thinly
sliced thin
1–2 tablespoons chopped garlic
1 teaspoon dried oregano
2 tablespoons olive oil
Salt and pepper, to taste

Directions:

Pastry

Combine flour, salt, and sugar in food processor. Add butter and
combine until it reaches the consistency of a coarse crumble.
With machine running, add water through the tube, processing
until pastry rolls off the sides into a ball. Cover and refrigerate
dough for 30 minutes. Roll out dough to fit tart pan or pie pan.

Filling

Preheat oven to 400°F. Brush mustard evenly over the bottom
of pastry shell. Top the mustard with the mozzarella, completely
covering the bottom. Arrange the tomato slices in overlapping
concentric rings. Sprinkle top with garlic, oregano, salt, and pepper. Drizzle with olive oil. Put tart pan on baking sheet and bake
for about 40 minutes.

Scrumptious Grilled Vegetable Platter

Courtesy of www.ILoveEggplant.com

Ingredients:

3 tablespoons olive oil
¼ cup balsamic vinegar
1 teaspoon dried parsley
1 teaspoon dried oregano
½ teaspoon dried thyme
1 tablespoon minced garlic
1 teaspoon chicken bouillon
¼ teaspoon black pepper
2 tomatoes, cut in ½-inch slices
1 medium eggplant, cut into
½-inch rounds

2 cups Portabella mushrooms,
sliced in ½-inch wedges
1 large zucchini, cut in ¼-inch
slices
2 bell peppers, sliced in ½-inch
strips
1 onion, cut in ½-inch rings

Directions:

Preheat grill to medium-high heat. Combine oil, vinegar, herbs, chicken bouillon, and pepper in a bowl and mix well. Add vegetables, mixing well to ensure all are coated with the marinade. Let stand for 30 minutes, mixing occasionally.

Arrange vegetable pieces on the grill, reserving leftover marinade in bowl. Keep turning every 4–5 minutes until cooked on both sides, brushing with leftover marinade as they cook. Serve as an appetizer or as a vegetable side with your favorite pasta.

Caprese Salad

Courtesy of Mariquita Farm
(www.mariquita.com)

Ingredients:

3 pounds heirloom tomatoes
20–30 leaves basil
1 pound mozzarella, cubed
Salt and freshly ground pepper, to taste

Directions:

Chop one or more ripe heirloom tomatoes. Add chopped fresh basil. Add some cubed fresh mozzarella. Drizzle with a little olive oil and season to taste with salt and pepper.

Bruschetta

Courtesy of Monica Musetti-Carlin, as seen in
Country Comfort: Summer Favorites
Serves 4-8

Ingredients:

Topping

8 plum tomatoes, skinned and diced or 24 cherry tomatoes, diced
1 clove garlic, crushed
1 tablespoon extra-virgin olive oil
1 teaspoon balsamic vinegar
12–16 basil leaves, finely chopped
1 pound fresh mozzarella cheese, sliced thin

Toasted Rounds of Bread

1 large loaf of Italian bread or French baguette
¼ cup extra-virgin olive oil
Sea salt and freshly ground green peppercorns, to taste

Directions:

Mix together tomatoes, garlic, olive oil, balsamic vinegar, and basil leaves, and set aside. Slice the mozzarella cheese into extra thin, round slices, and set aside. Cut your bread into the thin slices and brush with olive oil on one side. Place face-down on a baking sheet, and then place in a preheated 450°F oven for about 5 minutes or until they brown slightly. Take out, turn over, and salt and pepper the olive oil side. Place the mozzarella on each slice of bread, and top with the tomato-basil mixture. Serve immediately. Extra ingredients can be refrigerated for future use, but there are rarely leftovers.

Warm Roasted Tomato Bruschetta

Courtesy of the Central New York Tomatofest, from the kitchen
of Nadine Vande Walker
(www.cnytomatofest.org)

Ingredients:
Topping

4–5 medium fresh tomatoes,
diced
¾ cup diced red and green
peppers
¾ cup diced onions
2 cloves sliced garlic
2 tablespoons extra-virgin
olive oil
2 teaspoons kosher salt
1 teaspoon fresh ground
pepper
1 teaspoon sugar

¼ teaspoon crushed red
pepper flakes
2 tablespoons fresh sliced
basil, divided
1 tablespoon freshly grated
Parmesan cheese

Toasted Bread

1 fresh baguette loaf
½ cup garlic butter (purchase
or make your own)

Directions:
Topping

Preheat oven to 425°F.

Spread out the first four ingredients on a cookie sheet or stone-
ware bar pan. Drizzle with the olive oil and add salt, pepper,
sugar, red pepper, and 1 tablespoon of basil. Roast the tomatoes
and vegetables for 30 to 40 minutes until the tomatoes, peppers, and onions are tender and a little brown around the edges
and all liquid has evaporated (the consistency should be a little
thick). Place the tomato mixture in a bowl and top with remaining fresh basil and freshly grated Parmesan cheese. Place bowl
onto a serving plate with toasted bread.

Toasted Bread

Slice baguette in half and spread garlic butter on both sides of
the bread. Place bread under broiler for 3–5 minutes, until butter is melted and bread is slightly browned around the edges.
Slice and serve with warm tomato mixture.

Guacamole

Courtesy of Monica Musetti-Carlin, as seen in
Country Comfort: Summer Favorites
Serves 6-8

Ingredients:

1 tablespoon sea salt
1 cup red onion, chopped
2 tablespoons jalapeños, seeded and chopped
3 tablespoons fresh cilantro leaves, chopped
6 ripe avocados, chopped
¾ cup fresh tomatoes, seeded, chopped, and drained
Fresh lime juice, to taste

Directions:

Mix all the ingredients in a large bowl, cover, and chill before
serving.

Tabouleh

Courtesy of Monica Musetti-Carlin, as seen in
Country Comfort: Harvest

Ingredients:

3 tablespoons bulgur wheat
½ medium onion, chopped
1 teaspoon salt
½ teaspoon allspice
1 pound medium tomatoes, finely chopped
3 cups flat leaf parsley, minced
½ cup mint leaves, chopped fine
⅛ cup extra-virgin olive oil
Juice of 1 large lemon

Directions:

Prepare the bulgur, softening in warm water for 10 minutes.
Drain and set aside.

Mix onion with the salt and allspice.

Combine bulgur, onion, tomatoes, parsley, mint, oil, and lemon
juice in a large bowl. Refrigerate until ready to serve.

There are several combinations of basic herbs and spices har-
vested in the fall that are specific to certain international cuisine. Here are just a few highlights that can turn any dish into
something far more exciting in minutes:

Greek: cloves, Greek oregano, mint, parsley

Indian: curry, turmeric, coriander, cardamom

Mexican: chili powder, cumin, cilantro

Chinese: ginger, garlic, scallions

Middle Eastern: allspice and nutmeg

Roasted Tomato and Shallot Marmalade

Courtesy of Chef Therese Harding, The Classic Catering People

www.classiccatering.com

Yields 1 jar

Ingredients:

1 cup plum tomatoes, diced and seeded
3 tablespoons olive oil, divided
1 teaspoon brown sugar
1 cup shallots, diced
1 tablespoon balsamic syrup (see recipe below)
Sea salt and freshly cracked black pepper, to taste

Directions:

Preheat an oven to 310°F.

In a small bowl, toss plum tomatoes with 2 tablespoons of olive oil and brown sugar.

In a separate small bowl, toss shallots with the remaining 1 tablespoon of olive oil.

On a sheet pan, slowly roast the tomatoes for 40 minutes. On a separate sheet pan, slowly roast the shallots for 30 minutes. The vegetables should be translucent when finished.

Cool the vegetables to room temperature. Add 1 tablespoon of balsamic syrup to shallots.

Combine the shallots and tomatoes; season with salt and pepper.

Balsamic Syrup

Makes 1/3 cup

1 cup balsamic vinegar

Pour vinegar into a small, heavy, non-reactive saucepan. Bring to a boil over high heat; reduce by ⅓ (about 14 minutes). Cool in the pan. Pour into a small glass jar, cover, and store at room temperature.

Garden Fresh Salsa

Courtesy of Mary Elizabeth Roarke, as seen in
Country Comfort: Summer Favorites
Serves 6–8

Ingredients:

50 grape tomatoes, chopped
1 bunch fresh cilantro, chopped
1 onion, chopped
1 cup fresh lime juice
1 teaspoon each sea salt and freshly cracked black pepper
6 jalapeño rings, diced (optional)

Directions:

Mix all the ingredients in a large bowl, cover, and chill before
serving.

Marinara Sauce

Courtesy of Mary Elizabeth Roarke, as seen in
Country Comfort: Summer Favorites
Serves 6

Ingredients:

3 tablespoons extra-virgin
olive oil
2 small onions, chopped
1 garlic clove, minced
2½ cups Roma tomatoes,
peeled, seeded, and diced
½ tablespoon fresh oregano,
finely chopped (or ½ teaspoon
dried oregano, crumbled)

¼ teaspoon sugar
1 fresh basil leaf or a pinch of
dried basil, crumbled
Sea salt and freshly cracked
black pepper, to taste

Directions:

Heat oil in heavy medium-size saucepan over medium heat. Add
onions and garlic, and sauté until translucent (about 10 minutes). Add tomatoes, oregano, sugar, and basil. Simmer until
thickened for about 1 hour, stirring occasionally. Season with
salt and pepper to taste.

Tomato Ketchup

Courtesy of Mariquita Farm

(www.mariquita.com)

Makes 6 pints

Ingredients:

12½ pounds ripe tomatoes

2 medium onions

¼ teaspoon cayenne pepper

2 cups cider vinegar

1½ tablespoons broken stick cinnamon

1 tablespoon whole cloves

3 cloves garlic, finely chopped

1 tablespoon paprika

1 cup sugar

2½ teaspoons salt

Directions:

Wash and slice tomatoes. Place in pot and fill with enough water to just cover tomatoes. Boil until soft. Slice the onions and place them into another pot. Cover with a small quantity of water and cook until tender. Run the cooked onions and tomatoes through a sieve. Mix the onion and tomato pulp. Add the cayenne pepper. Boil this mixture rapidly until it has been reduced to about half of its original volume. Place vinegar in an enamel pan; add a spice bag containing the cinnamon, cloves, and garlic. Allow to simmer for about 30 minutes, then bring to a boil. Place cover on pan and remove from heat. Allow this to stand in covered pan until ready to use.

When tomato mixture has cooked down to half of its original volume, add spice mixture (of which there should be about 1 ¼ cups). Add the paprika, sugar, and salt and boil rapidly until thick (about 10 minutes). When finished, can to preserve (see next page).

To preserve ketchup, you will need canning jars with lids, a large pot (such as a boiling water canning pot or Dutch oven), and a wire rack that fits in the bottom of the pot. Warm the jars with simmering water or by running them through the dishwasher to prevent cracking. While still boiling, pour the ketchup into the sterilized jars, leaving ½ inch of empty space at the tops of the jars. Put on the caps and screw bands firmly tight. Prepare a water bath by laying the metal rack in the pot and filling the pot with enough water to cover the jars by 1 to 2 inches. Bring to a boil. Carefully lower the full jars into the pot and cover. Process in the boiling water bath for 5 minutes. Remove jars and check to make sure they are tightly sealed.

Resources

Aegean Café
www.sayvilleaegeancafe.com

American Grassfed Association
www.americangrassfed.org

British Tomato Growers' Association
www.britishtomatoes.co.uk

Central New York Tomatofest
www.cnytomatofest.org

Champagne® Mango
www.champagnemango.com

Christine Gable, Queen of the Quick Meal
www.quickmealhelp.com

The Court of Two Sisters
www.courtoftwosisters.com

Darcy's Delights
www.darcysdelights.com

Florida Tomato Committee
www.floridatomatoes.org

George Martin: The Original

www.georgemartingroup.com

Greensgrow Farms

www.greensgrow.org

ILoveEggplant.com

www.ILoveEggplant.com

La Tavola Restaurant

www.latavolasayville.com

Maggiano's "Little Italy"

www.maggianos.com

Mariquita Farm

www.mariquita.com

National Dairy Council

www.nationaldairycouncil.org

National Pasta Association

www.Ilovepasta.org

Red Fire Farm

www.redfirefarm.com

A Silverware Affaire

www.asilverwareaffair.net

Also in the *Farmstand Favorites* Series:

Farmstand Favorites: Apples
978-1-57826-358-5

Farmstand Favorites: Berries
978-1-57826-375-2

Farmstand Favorites: Cheese & Dairy
978-1-57826-395-0

Farmstand Favorites: Garlic
978-1-57826-405-6

Farmstand Favorites: Honey
978-1-57826-406-3

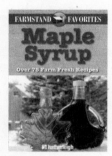

Farmstand Favorites: Maple Syrup
978-1-57826-369-1

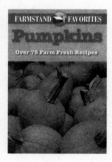

Farmstand Favorites: Pumpkins
978-1-57826-357-8